^ TER AND M^

In *Meter and Meaning*, poet Thomas Carper and scholar Derek Attridge join forces to present an illuminating user-friendly way to explore the rhythms of poetry in English.

The authors begin by showing the value of performing any poem aloud, so that we can sense its unique use of rhythm. From this starting point they suggest an entirely fresh, jargon-free approach to reading poetry. Illustrating their "beat-offbeat" method with a series of revealing exercises, they help us to appreciate the use of rhythm in poems of all periods and to understand the vital relationship between meter and meaning. Beginning with the very basics, this book enables a smooth progression to an advanced knowledge of poetic rhythms.

This is the essential guide to meter for anyone who wants to study, write, better appreciate or simply enjoy poetry. Thomas Carper and Derek Attridge make studying meter a pleasure and reading poetry a revelation.

Thomas Carper is the author of three volumes of metrical poetry: *Fiddle Lane*, *From Nature*, and *Distant Blue*, the recipient of the 2003 Richard Wilbur Award. He is Professor Emeritus of English at the University of Southern Maine. **Derek Attridge** is Professor of English at the University of York, England. He is the author of the highly influential texts on beat prosody, *The Rhythms of English Poetry* and *Poetic Rhythm: An Introduction*, and has also published books on literary theory, sixteenth-century poetry and twentieth-century fiction.

"This is a splendidly useful and elegantly thought-out introduction to the understanding of the rhythmic fabric of poetry in English, and to the way in which rhythmic patterns and effects become part of the very substance of what poetry says, rather than some kind of accompaniment to it. The authors have deployed sophisticated linguistic knowledge, literary sensitivity and poetic insight in the most clear and simple language possible, and their sample analyses are immediately comprehensible and enlightening. Anyone interested in poetry should acquire the knowledge so beautifully imparted here."

John Hollander, Yale University

"This is far and away the most accessible, effective and enjoyable introduction to meter I have ever come across. I have nothing but admiration for what the authors have done."

Rob Pope, Oxford Brookes University

"Many handbook approaches to scansion are Procrustean, beginning with metrical patterns and imposing them, like cookie-cutters, on lines of verse. Carper and Attridge start instead with the particular poem, sensitively read and spoken, and describe its wished rhythms in a vocabulary of 'three kinds of beat and five kinds of offbeat.' That vocabulary, which is not hard to learn, can well express all degrees of emphasis and pause, and by the time this fine book arrives at a discussion of our traditional measures, the reader has been prepared to see the infinite suppleness and subtlety which meter can have in the right hands."

Richard Wilbur, U.S. Poet Laureate, 1987–8

"A lively and engaging but also absolutely authoritative introduction to meter in English poetry. The book presents its concepts and method with conviction and panache."

Hans Bertens, University of Utrecht

"My students used this book and read it thoroughly and carefully. We then applied the 'beat-offbeat' approach to other pieces of poetry. And the result was phenomenal. A new light shone on the experience of reading poetry."

Warren Neal, Sacopee Valley High School

"This is the best introduction to poetic metre that I have seen."

Vicki Bertram, Nottingham Trent University

METER AND MEANING

AN INTRODUCTION TO RHYTHM IN POETRY

Thomas Carper and Derek Attridge

Routledge
Taylor & Francis Group

NEW YORK AND LONDON

First published 2003

Simultaneously published in the UK, USA and Canada
by Routledge
29 West 35th Street, New York, NY 10001
and Routledge
11 New Fetter Lane, London EC4P 4EE

Routledge is an imprint of the Taylor & Francis Group

© 2003 Thomas Carper and Derek Attridge

Typeset in Galliard by
Keystroke, Jacaranda Lodge, Wolverhampton
Printed and bound in Great Britain by
Biddles, Guildford and King's Lynn

Library of Congress Cataloging in Publication Data
Carper, Thomas
  Meter and meaning : an introduction to rhythm in poetry / Thomas
Carper and Derek Attridge.
     p. cm.
  1. English language—Versification. 2. English language—Rhythm.
I. Attridge, Derek. II. Title.
  PE1505.C36 2003
  821.009—dc21

                                    2003011927

British Library Cataloguing in Publication Data
A catalogue record for this book is available from the
British Library

ISBN 0–415–31174–8 (hbk)
ISBN 0–415–31175–6 (pbk)

CONTENTS

ACKNOWLEDGMENTS

The authors would like to thank the publishers and copyright holders for permission to reprint the following poems:

"Dream Variations" from *The Collected Poems of Langston Hughes* by Langston Hughes. © 1994 by The Estate of Langston Hughes. Used by permission of Alfred A. Knopf, a division of Random House, Inc. and David Higham Associates.

"Frost at Midnight" from *Sunday Skaters* by Mary Jo Salter. © 1994 by Mary Jo Salter. Used by permission of Alfred A. Knopf, a division of Random House, Inc.

"The Rites for Cousin Vit" from *Selected Poems* by Gwendolyn Brooks. Reprinted by consent of Brooks Permissions.

"My Papa's Waltz" from *Collected Poems of Theodore Roethke* by Theodore Roethke. © 1942 by Hearst Magazines, Inc. Used by permission of Doubleday, a division of Random House, Inc.

"Burnt Norton" from *Four Quartets* in *Collected Poems 1909–1962* by T. S. Eliot. Reprinted by permission of Faber & Faber.

"The Train" from *Hay* by Paul Muldoon. Reprinted by permission of Faber & Faber and Paul Muldoon.

"One Art" from *The Complete Poems: 1927–1979* by Elizabeth Bishop. © 1979, 1983 by Alice Helen Methfessel. Reprinted by permission of Farrar, Straus & Giroux, LLC.

"Neighbors" by Michelle Guerard.

"I Died for Beauty" and "I Like a Look of Agony" from *The Poems of Emily Dickinson* by Emily Dickinson. © 1951, 1955, 1979 by the President and Fellows of Harvard College. Reprinted by permission of the publishers and the Trustees of Amherst College.

We owe thanks to many people and institutions, and can name only a few.

Thomas Carper is grateful to his students at the University of Southern Maine who, over the years, shared their poetic experiences in creative writing and literature classes, and to Warren Neal of the English Department at Sacopee Valley High School, who kindly tried out *Meter and Meaning* in his Advanced Placement English class, where students learned to discuss rhythms easily and where the poets among them gained confidence in their ability to write metrically.

Derek Attridge wishes to thank the students at the University of Southampton, Strathclyde University, and Rutgers University whose discussions helped him develop the approach to meter embodied in this book, and the Leverhulme Trust for the research award which made it possible to find time to complete the project.

We are grateful to the poets, teachers, and scholars who reviewed the manuscript anonymously and offered helpful comments and suggestions, and to Liz Thompson, our editor, who provided both encouragement and constructive criticism.

To our wives, Janet and Suzanne, we owe more than words, metrical or unmetrical, can express.

T. C., D. A.

Cornish, Maine, U.S.A
York, England

INTRODUCTION

The aim of this book is to increase your enjoyment and understanding of English poetry written in regular meters. You may be a writer of poetry who would like to improve your grasp of metrical forms in English so that you may use them effectively in your poems. Perhaps you are studying literature in a high school or secondary school, or in a college or university, and would like to deepen your appreciation of the poetry you are reading. You may be a teacher who would like to provide your students with useful tools to help them discuss the rhythms of poems, and how they relate to other aspects of poetry. Or you may be one of the many people who are not specialists in literature or poetry but who love the sounds and rhythms of metrical poems and want to become even more aware of their pleasures and powers. This book is addressed to you.

Increased understanding, we believe, leads to increased enjoyment, but in the case of poetry, understanding is not only an intellectual matter. To experience a poem fully is to hear and feel it at the same time as responding to the meanings of its words and sentences, and to do this one has to be able to appreciate its rhythms. An invaluable tool in doing so, and in communicating one's experience to others, is a way of marking the lines of verse to indicate how the rhythm is working – in the case of metrical poetry, both how it uses familiar rhythms and how it creates particular effects by departing from these rhythms. We have attempted to make this process – scansion – as simple as possible by linking it directly to the way poems are experienced, and by using a straightforward set of symbols to mark the lines. We want to demystify meter, which for too long has been the preserve of the specialist, and we hope to add further dimensions to your appreciation of the art of the poets who, now as in the past, find heightened powers of communication and fresh possibilities for the expression of emotion through the use of regular, yet varied, rhythms.

The very words "scansion" and "prosody" – the metrical analysis of verse – cause anxiety for many lovers of poetry, and particularly for students young and old, from the early years of study to graduate schools. Examining the technical features of an attractive line seems to many like breaking a butterfly upon a wheel, to borrow a phrase from Alexander Pope, or, in the words of William Wordsworth, like murdering to dissect. Many feel that little is gained by dividing up lines of beautiful and moving language and then giving the little units, called "feet," names like iamb, trochee, anapest, dactyl, spondee, pyrrhic, amphibrach, ionic; the list of Greek-based labels goes on. If you are emotionally touched by the thoughts and rhythms of metrical poetry, this activity may seem no more than an intellectual game – and, often, a guessing game at that.

But if the perception of rhythms and meters is a physical as well as an intellectual act, why have such emphasis on *naming feet* when we sense the presence of meter by *feeling* it when we perform poems, either aloud or silently?

Before trying to answer these questions in the chapters that follow, we think it's important to say a little about who we are and why we believe this subject to be one that repays the expenditure of time and effort – both yours and ours. The "we" in this book usually means Tom Carper and Derek Attridge, not the "we" encountered in statements like "we know that, on this round planet, somewhere the sun is shining" or "here we sense the poet's melancholy." You, as reader and performer, will discover that we invite your own opinions and responses – agreeing or disagreeing – when we ask you to try out and evaluate our ways of performing certain metrical lines and identifying their rhythmic features, along with the meanings these rhythmic features help create.

We have both lived with poetry all our lives, teaching many hundreds of poems to large numbers of students, in Britain, the United States, and elsewhere. One of us has published several collections of metrical poetry, the other has published three books on the subject of rhythm and meter. We have also read a mountain of books and articles trying to introduce students to the way rhythm and meter work in poetry, and have always been disappointed – too many lists of terms, too much attention to norms and exceptions, too little examination of the basic assumptions about the experience of poetry underlying the discussion. We have always found this way of talking about meter left at least half of the students puzzled about what was going on, and this seemed a shame. The students were all thoughtful and dedicated, but the system of feet and their stress markings seemed to bear no relation to the expertise they demonstrated when reading poetry aloud. They could *perform* lines and entire poems beautifully, bringing out the beat of complex rhythms in just the way we would or, even better, with different emphases that exposed new meanings – often deeper meanings than we had noticed, or felt.

So we have for a long time been using a different approach in teaching metrical poetry, one for which there has been no classroom text. It is based on a simple principle: **Rhythm in English poetry is realized by the alternation of beats and offbeats**. We continued to use some of the traditional labels like "iambic pentameter" in talking about the way we performed poetry by reading it aloud, and our experience of its rhythms as we did so. The difference was that we did this not in a world of intellectual manipulations but in a world of felt perceptions. We helped our students *feel* metrical verse as poets would wish, in whole lines, not fragments of lines.

By developing a simple method of scansion based on beats and offbeats we enabled our students to discuss clearly with us and with each other the experience of rhythm that is integral to the perception of meanings and emotions in the metered poems that make up the largest part of British, American, and other poetries written in the English language. Some students went on to study the rhythms of poetry more extensively, and to gain familiarity with the traditional foot-based approach to meter; but the ability to feel the beats remained crucial to their use of older types of scansion. The best way to grasp the working of the various feet with Greek names that you will encounter in many studies of poetry is by first getting a clear sense of the rhythmic patterns of beats and offbeats that are fundamental to the way regular verse is heard. Our way of talking about metrical verse has also proved useful in understanding and discussing much poetry that is not in regular meters (generally known as "free verse") since the familiar rhythms upon which meter is built often play a significant part in these more freely organized poems.

The way of talking about poems that we developed in our class-rooms – beat prosody – is being used more and more widely in education and in literary criticism; this short introduction to the rhythms of English metrical poetry presents it in an easy-to-grasp form. Although there is no rhythm without at least some suggestion of meaning, and in a successful poem the two always work inseparably together, we will simplify matters by concentrating at the beginning on the most basic rhythms, and using made-up verse that has no pretensions at being richly meaningful poetry. (You will see, however, that questions of meaning enter very quickly into the discussion.) Later, when we have introduced the most important elements of meter, we shall broaden our discussion to real poems – some famous, some little known – and invite you to use what you have learned about rhythm to perform them, to perceive and enjoy rhythm and meaning working together, and to articulate your experience in the simple terms of beat prosody. Our focus is not on methods of analysis but on poems: on the many ways they stir, move, delight, soothe, or excite us, and on the part that regular but always varied rhythms play in creating their powerful appeal.

BASIC RHYTHMS 1

We all live with rhythms. In fact, we live in and through rhythms – rhythms of walking, talking, breathing, swimming, writing. When our muscles are engaged in any continuous activity, they prefer to tense and relax rhythmically, in time to a regular beat. The songs we sing and the music we listen or dance to can move our bodies and linger in our minds because they use rhythms that arise from these elementary pulses. Rhythms in poetry work similarly, from the nursery rhymes we chanted as young children to the subtle language we hear in performances of Shakespeare. In this opening chapter, you will see (and more importantly hear and feel) how these basic rhythms, at the heart of all metrical poetry, do their work.

We'll start with four lines written in simple rhythms.

First poem

```
We won't talk of stress, ⮾
We won't talk of feet. ⮾
We'll talk about rhythm –⮾
We'll talk about beat. ⮾
```

There are more profound poems. But this one reveals in an uncomplicated way a principal point of our Introduction, that **Rhythm in English poetry is realized by the alternation of beats and offbeats**, so it will be useful as we begin looking into (and listening to) the way metrical poetry creates its rhythm, and the ways we hear those rhythms. Sometimes a person will say, "There is only one way to hear the rhythm in such-and-such a line." But another person may disagree. How can this happen?

Pretty easily, *in some circumstances* – but not in all circumstances. Our first example will demonstrate this. In "First Poem" you will discover that there are two lines which have alternative meters. To perform the lines in the alternative ways is to take a big step toward understanding how to *hear* and *feel* meters, and then recognize metrical norms.

We can tell you that when the lines were written, it didn't occur to the writer that there could be differing metrical ways of reading them; he wrote with a single rhythm in mind, or, more precisely, with a single rhythm playing on his pulses. But applying the principles we will be studying, you will see how he was wrong.

First, though, an important point: with every example in this book, you must speak the lines aloud. If we are to understand rhythm in poetry, we have to get physical with it, and the only way to do this is to mouth it and hear it.

So, say the following lines aloud:

```
We won't talk of stress,
We won't talk of feet.
```

Notice that you've emphasized certain words more than others. Which were they?

While writing the lines, our not-particularly-inspired poet was emphasizing "won't" in both lines, the word "stress" in the first line, and the word "feet" in the second line. For him, the lines went like this (we show emphasis by means of bold type):

```
We won't talk of stress,
We won't talk of feet.
```

This means the lines had two beats. Maybe your performance of the lines was just the same as his. But maybe it wasn't – in which case you had one of the following pairs of *three*-beat lines:

```
We won't talk of stress,
We won't talk of feet.
```

or

```
We won't talk of stress,
We won't talk of feet.
```

This is a significant moment: we see (or hear) plainly that certain lines can have three valid, natural-sounding, *different* performances. And we also notice that the differing performances influence meanings: the first performance emphasizes the things that we *won't* be doing; the second emphasizes that *we* won't be doing certain things – but maybe others will; the third is very emphatic, with the lines almost shouting to express opposition even to bringing up the matter of "stress" and "feet." (One hears such energetic expression at football games: "Block that kick!")

Let's now perform aloud the second pair of lines:

```
We'll talk about rhythm —
We'll talk about beat.
```

Are there three possibilities for this pair, as there were for the first pair of lines? Try them out, continuing with the patterns we've just established, one with two beats in each line, two with three beats. Do they all work?

```
We'll talk about rhythm —
We'll talk about beat.
```

and

```
We'll talk about rhythm —
We'll talk about beat.
```

and

```
We'll talk about rhythm —
We'll talk about beat.
```

What about the first of the three-beat versions of these lines? Why doesn't "**We'll** talk about **rhyth**m" work?

The answer is obvious. Nobody who speaks the English language with average fluency pronounces the word "about" as **a**bout. It's always **about**. So for this pair of lines, the only possibilities are the first and third versions.

But just how likely is it that our poet, while writing his brief verse, had the third version in mind? Try the four lines yourself with this rhythm:

```
We won't talk of stress,
We won't talk of feet.
We'll talk about rhythm —
We'll talk about beat.
```

Does it seem to you that it's necessary, when presenting this fairly tame message to a reader, to use this degree of energy? Or do you feel, as we do, that these words, when emphasized so much, become more rhythmical than meaningful? That they turn, in effect, toward jazz rhythms and music?

A question still remains, though. If the first two lines of our small example may be performed in three different ways, and if lines three and four may be performed in only two different ways – because the "about" way won't work – and if the over-emphatic, jazzy way of performing all four lines together seems unnatural, what can we suppose the writer wanted us to experience? Will we say that our poet has written a poem using two rhythms, or meters – that is, two three-beat lines followed by two two-beat lines? Or will we say that the poem is one which the writer expects to be performed with two beats in every line?

As we begin our study of rhythm, you may be inclined to insist, "It's a free country. I hear threes and twos, so my answer is number one." But we trust, with good reason, that after going through this brief book and performing the examples and listening to the differences you yourself are making, you will choose answer two.

Why? As will be demonstrated in the course of our discussion, poets who bother to write in regular rhythms – in meters – prefer to stick to the patterns they've established. It's part of the art. They work to avoid ambiguities of rhythm. They depend on regularity. And they do this so that when, from time to time, they do change the rhythm a little, or even a lot, the change will be noticed by the reader, or listener. And in this way a meaningful emotional effect can be created.

Here is an illustration of how a variation from the expected meter can cause an emotional reaction; it's a slight rewriting of the opening lines of what is probably the most famous American poem, "A Visit from Saint Nicholas," published anonymously in 1823. Try reading this aloud:

```
'Twas the night before Christmas, when all through
                                    the house
Not a creature was stirring — not even a mouse;
The stockings were hung with care
In hopes that St. Nicholas soon would be there.
```

Because the third line is too short, it's jarring, and for no important reason relating to meaning or feeling. Why then would the poet abruptly interrupt the metrical flow of the line to shock the reader into paying particular attention to the ordinary act of hanging up Christmas stockings? In all likelihood, if we were to see this in a book of poems, we would think, "This is a misprint. Something has been left out." But the author, reputedly Clement Clark Moore, has in fact respected both the pattern of four beats per line and the rhyming pattern that the first two lines set up; so in the real poem he gives us what we're expecting: "The stockings were hung *by the chimney* with care." And with our expectations fulfilled, we feel satisfied.

Let's move on now and perform the following lines aloud:

Second poem

```
Hickory dickory dock, 3
The verse ticks like a clock. 3
But when the clock unwinds, 3
Its mechanism grinds, 2
And it stops.
```

How did the first line go? How many beats? Most of us will get "**hick**-or-y **dick**-or-y **dock**." And so a three-beat rhythm is set up. But what if some people hear the word "hickory" as a two-syllable word – "**hick**-ry"? There are two common pronunciations for the word, so of course the two-syllable pronunciation is all right. But does it change the number of beats we hear? No, we still have three. And even if there is any doubt, the following lines (except for the last) will assure us that we have heard three beats, and that the poet intended them: "But **when** the **clock** un**winds**," and so on.

What does the first line mean? Hickory is a kind of tree, or its wood, or a switch made of this wood. But what is "dickory"? The question may seem odd, and the answer obvious: dickory is a nice-sounding word made up by somebody to add rhyme and rhythm to a children's poem. But notice, there is a point to be made here that can be applied to many devices of sound and rhythm we may encounter in the most sophisticated, even the most difficult, poems: often the pleasures to be gained from the *sounds* and *rhythms* of words are more important to the poet than the literal meanings of the words – in fact, the sounds and rhythms *create* meaning. Notice that the literal meaning of "hickory" really has no connection with the nursery rhyme, in which a mouse runs up a clock and then, when the clock strikes, runs back down again. Of course we can suppose, or even insist, that the clock must have been made of hickory; but in this case we must ask, which is greater, the pleasure of coming up with an impossible-to-prove "meaning," or the plea-sure of hearing pleasant, childlike sounds and rhythms working harmoniously together?

The second line can have two readings. Speak the line again, several times, and try to say what the two performances might be; then read on.

```
The verse ticks like a clock.
```

Here are the possibilities:

```
The verse ticks like a clock.
The verse ticks like a clock.
```

What's your preferred performance? The first is very regular, and so may be said to reflect the regular ticking of a clock. But perhaps you feel that as a line of verse it is a bit mechanical (like clocks, rather than poems). The second performance, with an emphasis on "ticks," seems more natural and "spoken" (at least to us), and also has more energy. Now if we were further along – if we were at the point of discussing scansion – we would agree that slightly different markings would be needed for the different ways of performing the line, whichever one you prefer. But for now, we can agree that there are three beats, and to get into the swing of the simple verse, that's all we need.

The third line is quite regular (an alternate performance that emphasizes "but" rather than "when" is possible though not likely):

> But **when** the **clock** un**winds**,

The regularity is no surprise, for a large proportion of lines in metrical poems will be very regular. Why? The poet knows that if there are too many irregularities, the meter will be lost.

The fourth line is quite regular, too; try saying it aloud:

> Its mechanism grinds,

You will feel two strong beats:

> Its **mech**anism **grinds**,

But wait. We've been saying all along that three beats is the norm, the regular pattern, for this poem. Where is that third beat which can be felt, but that isn't so strong?

> Its **mech**anism **grinds**,

This is another significant moment. The reader has been rolling rhythmically through the poem, and so feels the beat continuing even when the "-is-" in "mechanism" gets nowhere near the emphasis that "mech-" and "grinds" get. Thus the line fits perfectly into the expected three-beat pattern, even though the "-is-" is a gentle pat rather than a thump.

And our last line?

> And it stops.

Two beats, maybe? Or one? Take your pick.

So far we have touched on several important points: that in certain circumstances a single line can have different metrical performances; that poets writing metrically tend to stick to their established patterns;

and that it is possible to feel beats on parts of words that have no special emphasis. In Chapters 2 and 3 we will introduce a method of scansion that will make these points even clearer and easier to understand.

Third poem

Whose woods these are I think I know.

Whose words these are perhaps you know.
They're Frost's, who wrote them long ago.

Again we ask you to perform the lines, naturally but with energy. How many beats do you feel? The norm of our first poem was two beats. Then, we gave you a poem with a three-beat norm. And now?

Whose **words** these **are** per**haps** you **know.**

Yes, it's a four-beat line, a variation on the opening of "Stopping by Woods on a Snowy Evening," a poem published in 1923 by the American poet Robert Frost. (We will look at the complete poem in Chapter 2.) Frost's poem has a generally calm and steady four-beat meter, and in these Third Poem lines there is that same regularity (although without Frost's marvelous language).

Even here, though, many people are likely to perform the line with no particular emphasis on "are." That would leave only three prominent beats.

Whose **words** these are per**haps** you **know.**

But if you listen and feel, the four-beat rhythm that structures the line will be perceived to give a pat, if not a thump, to "are." And if there is any question about the poem's meter – three-beat or four-beat? – the second line will confirm the sense of the poem's intended four-beat norm.

They're **Frost's,** who **wrote** them **long ago.**

It's useful to remember that a poem's larger context is usually a dependable guide for determining the meter of individual lines because, as we have said, poets writing metrically tend to stick to patterns.

Two-, three-, and four-beat lines like the ones we've asked you to look at and listen to occur in thousands of poems, but one of the most common lines in metrical poems written in English is the five-beat line. So we'll now give you several five-beat lines about a very famous five-beat-line poem.

Fourth poem

How do I love thee? Let me count the ways.

Elizabeth Barrett Browning counted ways
She loved her poet-husband. We can hear
The ways she counted beats, so that her praise
Would come as music to our inner ear.

Here we encounter the meter that has been the most common one for serious poetry in English since the late 1300s, when Chaucer wrote his *Canterbury Tales*. In every century since that time, poets writing metrically have used this five-beat line, which has tradition-ally been called **"iambic pentameter."** (More information about conventional names for poetic lines and meters, together with a glossary of other technical terms, will be found in Chapter 6: "Names and labels.") William Shakespeare, John Milton, Anne Bradstreet, Alexander Pope, John Keats, Elizabeth Barrett Browning, Robert Frost, Gwendolyn Brooks: these are only a few of those men and women who have enriched poetry in English with poems written in this most flexible and natural-sounding line.

Perhaps you are already familiar with a poem called "How Do I Love Thee? Let Me Count the Ways," which Elizabeth Barrett Browning (1806–61) included in a collection, entitled *Sonnets from the Portuguese*, addressed to her husband, the poet Robert Browning. As we will discuss in a later chapter, "How Do I Love Thee?" achieves harmony and a sense of conviction in large part by means of its formal dignity and artistic control of intense emotion, to which the five-beat meter makes an important contri-bution.

Though our example, our Fourth Poem, is short on passion, it can help to illuminate the five-beat rhythm and some of the ways in which that rhythm may be manipulated to create variety and energy. Let's speak the entire Fourth Poem aloud.

```
Elizabeth Barrett Browning counted ways
She loved her poet-husband. We can hear
The ways she counted beats, so that her praise
Would come as music to our inner ear.
```

First, notice that there's a big difference between how you've moved from line to line in our earlier three poems and how you move from line to line in this poem. You will remember, or you can look back and see, that in "We won't talk of stress," in "Hickory dickory dock," and in "Whose words these are perhaps you know" there was, at the end of every line, a natural pause, as a complete sentence or phrase would finish with a comma, period, or dash. But in Fourth Poem we have . . . what?

If you try reading our Fourth Poem quite fast, rushing from line to line, you may very well feel what you're experiencing is prose, or almost prose – that written out it would look like this:

```
Elizabeth Barrett Browning counted ways she loved her
poet-husband. We can hear the ways she counted beats,
so that her praise would come as music to our inner
ear.
```

Although a few readers may pick up hints of a five-beat rhythm, this paragraph, when performed, will be experienced by most as what we all expect ordinary paragraphs to be: prose.

But if a poet wants us to perform poems this way – rushing over the line endings and pausing only at punctuation – why does he or she bother to have lines at all? It takes work and some skill to write a line that is both metrical and natural sounding; if prose can do the whole job, why make life more difficult?

The whole job of poetry is more, though, than to make the kinds of "meaning" we look for in prose. As the last line of our example suggests, the job of poetry is to make a music of language – an enlarged experience rather than an experience entirely summed up by "just the facts." And our Fourth Poem gives some hints of how it can be done.

Perform the first two lines again. How do you hear them? Where do you hear their beats? This is one possible performance:

```
Elizabeth Barrett Browning counted ways
She loved her poet-husband. We can hear
```

Did you find yourself pausing, just a little bit, after "ways" to mark the line's end and prevent the prose effect we've just noticed as a possibility? If so, good. To observe a poet's line breaks does justice to his or her art and effort. On the other hand, was there a big thump on "ways" – a breaking-off of the sentence and its meaning – and a longish pause following? If so, consider a more natural sort of speech in your performance. Pause a bit, but move on. Rewards in pleasure and understanding will come if you do.

Perhaps for some performers a few of the beats in these lines, like the "po-" in "poet" or the "we" in the second line, may have been more pats than thumps. That's just fine, for there is still a sense that the lines have their expected five beats, in this case felt regularly on every other syllable – except for the first word of our poem. Something is different about that word "Elizabeth." If you look at the syllables closely, you will notice that there are two of them between the beats in the words "Elizabeth" and "Barrett": "E-liz-a-beth **Bar**-rett." Nevertheless, this slight difference from the regularity that can be experienced in the rest of the first line, and in the entire second line, does not interfere with the hearing of five beats. Instead, there is a light, extra syllable that adds a bit of interest to the first line's music. You can hear and feel the difference between our original version and a revision where a shorter first name noticeably changes the line's rhythm and effect, making it more thumpingly metrical:

```
Elizabeth Barrett Browning counted ways
Cassandra Barrett Browning counted ways
```

How do you hear the third line? Here are two possibilities. Try them out. Which version sounds more natural to you? More energetic?

```
1. The ways she counted beats, so that her praise

2. The ways she counted beats, so that her praise
```

There is a choice between a very regular placing of the five beats in performance 1, or a varied placing in performance 2, with emphasis on the "so" rather than the "that." Either performance is acceptable, though we like performance 2 because for us the emphasis on "so" arouses more anticipation to hear the reason for the poet's counting beats.

In line four, there are again five beats, but one of them is on a word that doesn't call for any emphasis – "to":

Would **come** as **music** **to** our **in**ner **ear.**

Although it would sound very odd – artificial and mechanical – to give "to" the same kind of thump as the other syllables with beats, it is still possible to *feel* the beat on it if the lines have been performed rhythmically and if the word is pronounced clearly, without slurring it into the next one.

In our next chapter, we will begin scanning these lines, and others, to provide more complete visual representations of the features of rhythmical verse that we have thus far been exploring.

FURTHER PRACTICE

The discussion you have just finished reading and participating in has, we hope, given you a good sense of basic rhythms. But you may wish to try your hand at additional exercises to enhance your skill and confidence. Here are several which have proven useful for those new to the exploration of rhythm in poetry.

1   Reading aloud in groups

This chapter has often asked you to speak lines aloud, sometimes in alternative ways, to become conscious of details in your own performances. But you may find it instructive to get together with several other people, or in a class, and recite metrical **stanzas** aloud – meaningfully, and not timidly. You will discover that this "choral reading" will cause you to adjust your pronunciation in order to conform to the shared expectations of the group. When this happens, the underlying structure of beats becomes unmistakable.

Why? Because as individual performances are submerged in the larger group to create a unified effect, the pulse of the most basic pattern of beats is felt. This is a common experience at sporting events when random shouts become a chorus: "Aussie, Aussie, Aussie, Oi! Oi! Oi!"

Here are several poems to read aloud chorally. Listen as a single "committee" reading emerges, especially if you read them more than once. (In the "Further Practice" sections of Chapters 2 and 3 we'll return to these poems for more detailed discussion.)

The first is a short poetic version of part of Psalm 71, written by Mary Sidney, Countess of Pembroke (1561–1621). Many poets have attempted to put poems from the Hebrew Bible's Book of Psalms into regular English meters, and the Countess of Pembroke was one of the most innovative writers to do so in the sixteenth century.

> Lord, on thee my trust is grounded:
> Leave me not with shame confounded;
>   But in justice bring me aid.
> Let thine ear to me be bended;
> Let my life, from death defended,   5
>   Be by thee in safety stayed.

Our "committee" finds <u>four</u> emphasized syllables, or beats, in each line. Even though the typographical arrangement suggests that lines three and six should somehow be different, the basic meter is the same. The indentations are simply clues that lines three and six share the same rhyme: "aid" and "stayed" (meaning "sustained").

"The Lily," one of the *Songs of Experience* by the British poet and artist William Blake (1757–1827), has a similar rhythm. The two last lines may seem longer than the first two (they certainly look longer), but are they really of a different metrical length?

> The modest Rose puts forth a thorn:
> The humble Sheep, a threatening horn:
> While the Lily white, shall in Love delight,
> Nor a thorn nor a threat stain her beauty bright.

Here our "committee" finds that although there are a lot more syllables in the two concluding lines, there are only four on which we feel beats. In line three these are "Lil-," "white," "Love," and "-light"; in line four they are "thorn," "threat," "beaut-," and "bright."

You can of course experiment with choral readings of any number of metrical poems. But here as a final example is the poem whose concluding lines are carved at the base of the Statue of Liberty, a gift from France to the United States located on an island in New York harbor between the "twin cities" of New York and Newark; it's "The New Colossus" by Emma Lazarus (1849–87). It's helpful to know that the "old colossus," the Colossus of Rhodes, was a huge brass statue of the sun god whose legs, it was long believed, straddled the entrance to the harbor of the ancient Greek city of Rhodes.

```
Not like the brazen giant of Greek fame,
With conquering limbs astride from land to land;
Here at our sea-washed, sunset gates shall stand
A mighty woman with a torch, whose flame
Is the imprisoned lightning, and her name          5
Mother of Exiles. From her beacon-hand
Glows world-wide welcome; her mild eyes command
The air-bridged harbor that twin cities frame.
"Keep, ancient lands, your storied pomp!" cries she
With silent lips. "Give me your tired, your poor,  10
Your huddled masses, yearning to breathe free,
The wretched refuse of your teeming shore.
Send these, the homeless, tempest-tossed to me,
I lift my lamp beside the golden door!"
```

If your committee's reading emerges, perhaps after several recitations, with a five-beat norm, you're doing fine. But you're likely to discover that different people will initially be feeling those five beats in somewhat different places. This is not surprising.

In the next chapter's "Further Practice" section you can see one possible placing of the beats in these poems. Don't worry if our "words-with-the-beat" are not yours. After considering beats more fully, and then the offbeats that come between them, you will be able to return to this choral reading exercise and understand why certain differences are to be expected, and how those differences can reveal nuances in the poem's meaning.

2 Metrical walking and tapping

When walking down a corridor, or along the street, make up sentences (using nonsense words if you like) where there's an emphasized word or syllable for every step – and different words or syllables coming between the steps. Like this:

```
The cor-ri-dor is full of junk and I am feel-ing
    STEP      STEP     STEP      STEP      STEP STEP

pret-ty stu-pid as I try to make my way.
STEP      STEP     STEP STEP    STEP     STEP
```

Or, you can "walk" nursery rhymes or other metrical poems which you may have in your head – or which you can have on a piece of paper and "walk-read" aloud. For example:

```
Twink-le, twink-le, litt-le star,    4
STEP        STEP        STEP    STEP

How I wond-er what you are.
STEP  STEP    STEP     STEP
```

or

```
I lift my lamp be-side the gold-en door!
  STEP     STEP    STEP      STEP     STEP
```

Some "metrical walkers" like to feel that every first beat in five-beat lines will come consistently on the right foot (or the left). These people are happier when they add an "end of the line" step before moving on to the next line – like this, with the beats beginning with the right foot (Rf):

```
The wretch-ed ref-use of your teem-ing shore.
      Rf        Lf      Rf       Lf         Rf       Lf

Send these, the home-less, temp-est-tossed to me,
      Rf          Lf           Rf          Lf       Rf Lf

I lift my lamp be-side the gold-en door!"
  Rf       Lf      Rf        Lf       Rf       Lf
```

With this device you can walk through a great deal of five-beat verse, learning a lot about its underlying rhythm and also noticing those moments of surprise that will create significant meaning when the lines are not marched to, but spoken in a natural way.

If walking is difficult or impossible for you, a similar sort of exercise can be performed by tapping with your foot or finger, or with a pencil in your hand.

```
E-liz-abeth Bar-ratt Brown-ing count-ed ways
  TAP        TAP      TAP       TAP      TAP
```

Incidentally, in the early 1800s the English poet William Wordsworth would often compose his poems out loud while walking along village roads, where others would sometimes observe him. In lines 122 to 130 of the fourth book of his long autobiographical poem *The Prelude*, published after his death in 1850, he expresses gratitude that the dog accompanying him would always give "timely notice" (bark?) when others approached, so that the poet could become "normal" again and be prepared

```
To give and take a greet-ing that might save
   STEP      STEP  STEP       STEP      STEP

My name from pit-eous rum-ours, such as wait
   STEP       STEP     STEP      STEP   STEP

On men sus-pect-ed to be crazed in brain.
  STEP   STEP    STEP  STEP     STEP
```

Wordsworth doesn't specifically say that he stepped to his meters, but he does admit to murmuring and talking to himself while being "harassed with the toil of verse" – evidence of his physical involvement with poetry.

3 An annoying limerick

Here's a conventional limerick. Perhaps you've come across it before.

```
There once was a diner at Crewe
Who discovered a mouse in his stew.
    Said the waiter, "Don't shout
    And wave it about,
Or the rest will be wanting one too!"
```

Are there any metrical problems with reciting this aloud? Does it seem to you that it's metrically just fine? It does to us.

But what about this one, also familiar to many?

```
There once was a man from Japan
Whose limericks never would scan.
    When friends asked him why
    He replied with a sigh,
"Because I always try to put as many words in the
                last line as ever I possibly can."
```

All of us familiar with limericks know what that last line is supposed to be: something four-beat, like "I haven't learned yet – but I can!" So we get the joke when that last line is absolutely not metrical. We're surprised and amused.

Here's a question, though. In spite of knowing that you will fail to get that line into four beats however fast you rush through it (you can even *see* that it's impossible), do you want to make it fit the expected meter? Do you try to do it? Are you not only amused by the limerick, but a bit annoyed by it as well – because it doesn't play by the rules?

We can't answer this question for you, but bringing it up seems worthwhile – because, as will become evident in the chapters to come, a more subtle creation of surprise often generates vitality and enhances meaning in metrical poetry.

BEATS

B, b, [B]

2

In our preceding chapter you were asked to recite a number of metrical lines aloud and with energy. You compared your performances with ours. We discovered that most of the time there was agreement about the placing of the beats, but that some of us had slightly differing performances of individual lines with, naturally, slightly differing meanings. For of course in daily conversation our way of saying a sentence can change its meaning: "**I'll** never go there again" (but maybe someone else will); or "I'll never go **there** again" (because the place is awful). And, finally, we observed that some lines can be performed in more than one perfectly natural-sounding way that preserves the expected number of beats. In Chapter 1, then, we did what poets do when they write in meter: they listen for the beat.

Now we come to scansion, a useful device for noting down what the reader or performer experiences when he or she responds to the rhythm of a poem. Scanning a poem simply means showing on paper, through the use of a few clear, easily remembered signs, where the beats and offbeats are felt, and the patterns – quite a small number of patterns – that they produce. If a poem is written in a particular meter (as virtually all poetry in English of the past five hundred years is, and as a growing amount of contemporary poetry is), it's important to be sensitive to just what's happening with that aspect of the poet's performance, in the same way that it's important to be sensitive to subtleties of language and meaning. What we are going to present in this chapter is a simple way of noting down what people actually do when performing metrical poetry.

As we've already seen, the first part of a metrical line that people usually notice is the beats, so that's where we'll begin our scansion.

We looked in Chapter 1 at a First Poem that began, "We won't talk of stress." We discovered that the line could be said in three different ways – in one case with two beats and in two cases with three, as you will recall:

```
        We won't talk of stress,

        We won't talk of stress,

and     We won't talk of stress,
```

Here the beats were emphasized by the use of boldface type. The way our scansion – called beat scansion – indicates a word or part of a word that has an evident emphasis, and so may carry a beat, is by the use of a capital **B**. Here is the simple way we scan the line to indicate the beats in the three performances.

```
        We won't talk of stress,
           B               B

or      We won't talk of stress,
        B        B         B

or      We won't talk of stress,
           B     B         B
```

Using a single letter symbol we have indicated our three possible readings: the first, clearly enough, a two-beat line, the second and third three-beat lines.

What about the next line, with the beats scanned in the three ways? Again, simple enough:

```
        We won't talk of feet.
           B               B

or      We won't talk of feet.
        B        B         B

or      We won't talk of feet.
           B     B         B
```

You can do the next two lines by yourself:

```
We'll talk about rhythm —
We'll talk about beat.
```

We suggest that you write the lines out, mark them, and then compare your performances with ours, given below (p. 28). (Notice that we place the **B** under the first vowel of the syllable that carries the beat.)

Going on to our second poem, you will hear – and see – that it would have the easily recognized beats of its first line scanned this way:

```
Hickory dickory dock,
 B       B       B
```

And the second line in one of these two ways:

```
The verse ticks like a clock.
    B           B       B
```

or
```
      The verse ticks like a clock.
          B    B              B
```

And the third, a perfectly regular line:

```
But when the clock unwinds,
    B         B      B
```

And the fourth – but wait. We noticed that the "-is-" of "mechanism" carries the beat. How can we indicate that this beat is not a thump but a pat? Various ways have been devised for noting a beat that is *not* emphasized, but we will use a lower-case **b** – available on typewriters and computers, and written easily by hand. So we have this:

```
Its mechanism grinds,
 B    b      B
```

Three beats, as we know; and the letter B is there three times, though one of them is the pat (**b**) rather than the thump (**B**). (We will consider the final short line in the next chapter.)

We are, of course, talking about thumps and pats in a metaphorical way – nobody is putting a hand on anybody's shoulder, either heavily or lightly. But the metaphor works well enough because it calls attention to what the reader *feels*, and that's the important thing. As we go on it will become more evident that the context of a line provides the expectation of just how many beats we are likely to encounter: "Its mechanism grinds" will have three beats because it can naturally be heard with three beats, and because *every preceding line has had three beats*. A norm has been established and so we hear and feel what we expect to hear and feel.

In Chapter 1 we mentioned that there is an additional fact about poems written in lines with three easily recognized beats. If you pay very close attention to your physical experience, you may discover that in "Hickory dickory dock" the rhythm actually carries beyond the written lines; you may feel an extra beat, a "virtual beat" – [B] – that brings the total to four:

```
Hickory dickory dock
 B       B        B      [B]
```

After looking at four- and five-beat lines, we will see and hear how this unpronounced beat is particularly evident in poems written in **"ballad stanzas."**

But let's return to our pronounced **B**'s and **b**'s. Chapter 1's four-beat poem was modeled on the opening of a poem by Robert Frost. Here it is with its beats in bold type, then with the beats scanned:

```
Whose words these are perhaps you know.
They're Frost's, who wrote them long ago.

Whose words these are perhaps you know.
      B          B       B          B
They're Frost's, who wrote them long ago.
          B            B        B    B
```

If your performance gives less emphasis to "are," you will of course have a **b** instead of a **B** under that word. Either sounds natural enough.

Now it's time to turn to the real poem, Robert Frost's "Stopping by Woods on a Snowy Evening," which has four stanzas of four lines each. Here are the first two stanzas to read aloud:

```
Whose woods these are I think I know.
His house is in the village though;
He will not see me stopping here
To watch his woods fill up with snow.

My little horse must think it queer          5
To stop without a farmhouse near
Between the woods and frozen lake
The darkest evening of the year.
```

The four-beat norm is inescapable; and we can feel that the sense created of peacefulness and thoughtfulness is due not only to the description of the scene, and to the poet's musings, but also to the steady regularity of the four-beat rhythm. Now, having read aloud – that essential requirement for feeling and hearing the meter – do a second thing to become even more intimate with the poem and with its rhythm: *copy the eight lines out on a piece of paper.* Double or triple space. Listen to the words as you copy, making sure that you don't drop or add anything. (Scansion is wrecked if you don't copy accurately.)

Now that you have your own copy, and before reading on, put the **B**'s and **b**'s under the first vowels of those words or syllables that carry the beat.

With that done, we can now discuss the places where your scansion – or performance – and ours may differ, and just what the possibilities are. To start, here is our scansion of the lines:

```
Whose woods these are I think I know.
      B           b       B        B
His house is in the village though;
      B       b       B           B
He will not see me stopping here
 B           B       B        B
To watch his woods fill up with snow.
      B           B        B           B
```

```
My little horse must think it queer                    5
    B       B              B          B
To stop without a farmhouse near
    B      B       B          B
Between the woods and frozen lake
    B         B           B      B
The darkest evening of the year.
    B       B        b       B
```

How closely do you agree with us? Here are the lines where we'd expect to see other possibilities:

1: Under "are" a **B** instead of a **b**. Why not? – you would simply have a more emphatically metrical line. But with a little less emphasis on the "are" we give greater emphasis to "woods," the more important word. So we've preferred that performance.

2: Maybe you've put a **B** under "in." That would mean giving a lot of emphasis to the word – but does "in" really deserve it? Listen carefully to your own performance again; you might want to reconsider.

3: It's very likely that you put the **B** under "will" rather than "He." That's certainly acceptable. Notice, though, what our performance brings to the poem. With an emphasis on "He," the difference between the speaker and the man in the village is made more vivid: "He," being at home, is not concerned with woods on a snowy evening; he's a different sort of person from the one who stops to meditate on the loveliness and mystery of the scene. The metrical emphasis on the pronoun also suggests a connection between feelings in this stanza – where the poem's speaker seems disturbed to think that "He," the villager, might see him stopping – and the feelings in the next stanza, where the "little horse," who likewise prefers houses, must think that the speaker's pausing for a meditative moment is queer. What are your opinions?

4: Our performance is likely to be yours, though putting the **B** under "fill" rather than "up" is a possibility. Such a performance could give an even stronger sense of the snow actually burying the woods.

5: A very regular line; there aren't any natural-sounding alternatives.
6: Perhaps a **b** rather than a **B** under the "out" in "without" would indicate your way of saying the line. Incidentally, you may notice that the "house" part of "farmhouse" gets pretty much of a thump – perhaps nearly as much as the "farm" part. A North American pronunciation would be more likely to do this than a British one, but it's still not enough of a thump to attract a beat, which would break Frost's pattern by giving us five **B**'s in the line. It's not likely that he would have done it, so we won't either. (Later we will see how beat scansion can show nearly equal emphasis on "farm" and "house.")
7: Another perfectly regular line.
8: As with line two, we suggest that if you put a **B** rather than a **b** under "of," reconsider. A general rule is not to thump articles (*a*, *an*, *the*) and prepositions (*with*, *of*, *by*, *to*, and so on). In some circumstances, of course, general rules are broken; listening and feeling will tell you what to do.

A general observation about performing and marking beats: some performers, particularly beginners, indicate mostly strong beats – **B**'s – when scanning metrical verse in English. As they become more sensitive to their own practice, though, they tend to develop more nuanced readings which draw on the full resources of the spoken language – observing the beats but not giving them excessive emphasis. So try, then, to listen carefully and avoid over-emphatic performances which, like our "We **won't talk** of **stress**," become chant-like and move away from the tones of a speaking voice. In reciting nursery rhymes it's fine to emphasize every beat strongly – even those syllables that would be quite weak in normal speech. But poets writing metrical verse take advantage of the possibility of using unemphasized syllables for beats, and the most persuasive and moving performances reflect this.

These two stanzas from "Stopping by Woods on a Snowy Evening" are only half of the poem, and you may want to complete the scansion, so here is the text of stanzas 3 and 4, which you can copy out and use for marking beats. Then, you may compare your performance with ours, which is given later in the chapter (p. 28).

```
He gives his harness bells a shake
To ask if there is some mistake.                    10
The only other sound's the sweep
Of easy wind and downy flake.

The woods are lovely, dark and deep,
But I have promises to keep,
And miles to go before I sleep,                     15
And miles to go before I sleep.
```

By the way, when you do exercises like this, try to mark the beats quickly, at the moments you experience them when reading aloud. If you pause within lines and start staring at the words on the page, the physical activity of feeling the beats can become the visual or mental activity of working out a puzzle. It won't help at all, and it's a good way to complicate your life needlessly.

Now, having considered Frost's four-beat lines, we'll complete our scanning of the beats in our Chapter 1 verses by marking the beats in these five-beat lines with the **B**'s and **b**'s that match up with the emphasized and unemphasized syllables. Here is what we came up with first in the previous chapter:

```
Elizabeth Barrett Browning counted ways
She loved her poet-husband. We can hear
The ways she counted beats, so that her praise
Would come as music to our inner ear.
```

This performance of the four lines would be scanned as follows:

```
Elizabeth Barrett Browning counted ways
   B        B        B       B      B

She loved her poet-husband. We can hear
     B         B   B        B     B

The ways she counted beats, so that her praise
     B       B      B            B        B

Would come as music to our inner ear.
      B        B    b   B     B
```

But you will remember that the third line had an alternate perfor-
mance, which we see here:

The **ways** she **count**ed **beats, so** that her **praise**

This performance would be scanned with the third and fourth beats
heard in the words "beats" and "so":

```
The ways she counted beats, so that her praise
    B        B        B    B            B
```

Not complicated. But perhaps you have noticed that the basic rule
for meter in English poetry – that rhythm is realized by the alternation
of beats and offbeats – seems to be broken here, because we have two
B's together, with no syllable between them. (You may have even
noticed that our line "The verse ticks like a clock" could be performed
with beats coming side by side.) Don't worry. This chapter's concern
is only with beats. In the next chapter we will get to offbeats, and
when we do you will see that useful signs are available to show just
what is happening when our performances give us these kinds of
change in a line's rhythm, its music.

We have now discussed the meanings of **B** and **b** in scansion, and
how they provide visual representations of the rhythms discovered
by reading lines naturally and with energy. After discussing our
three-beat poem, though, we referred very briefly to an additional
beat symbol, the **[B]**, which is particularly useful in showing what
is happening rhythmically in an often-encountered stanza of verse,
the **"ballad stanza"** (also known as **"common meter"** or **"common
measure"**), where four-beat lines alternate with three-beat ones. To
hear and feel what's going on, perform aloud the following stanza
from a poem by the English poet Robert Herrick, who published
"To the Virgins, to Make Much of Time" in 1648:

> Gather ye rosebuds while ye may,
>   Old time is still a-flying;
> And this same flower that smiles today
>   Tomorrow will be dying.

Here's our performance, with its "visible" beats indicated by bold type:

```
Gather ye rosebuds while ye may,
   Old time is still a-flying;
And this same flower that smiles today
   Tomorrow will be dying.
```

Do you sense, as we do, that the second and fourth lines continue on metrically beyond the words that are read and spoken? Test the notion. Recite and compare Herrick's stanza with this altered version – which we've concocted:

```
Gather ye rosebuds while ye may,
   Old time is still a-flying on;
And this same flower that smiles today
   Tomorrow will be dead and gone.
```

Notice that when a poem has a very rhythmical four-beat line, one expects the next line to have four beats as well. That expectation is satisfied by our lengthened versions of Herrick's lines. But even the shorter lines which the poet originally wrote, where only three beats are "visible," the missing fourth beat is felt as an evident pause when the line is performed. With an extra beat occurring after "flying" and "dying," the number of experienced beats in all of the lines comes to four. When this beat is included in scansions, as is most usual with ballad stanzas, it is represented by [**B**]. We call this extra beat a **virtual beat**, because it isn't created directly by language but, instead, by our tendency to perceive simple rhythms in four-beat units.

```
Gather ye rosebuds while ye may,
  B        B        B       B
   Old time is still a-flying;
        B        B      B      [B]
And this same flower that smiles today
     B       B              B       B
   Tomorrow will be dying.
        B       b       B      [B]
```

Perhaps your performance, and scansion, had a few more **b**'s in the place of our **B**'s (as for "while" and "still"), and perhaps you gave more emphasis to "will" than we did. But the important thing to notice is that not only do the four-beat lines have their expected four **B**'s; the three-beat ones also have four beats – three spoken **B**'s plus the additional **[B]** that indicates the "beat without a word," or virtual beat, which is felt as a strong pause coming at the ends of the lines. (A composer setting this stanza to music would almost certainly take into account the virtual beats, perhaps by stretching out the last syllable of "a-flying" and "dying.")

Having discussed and practiced the scansion of beats in the kinds of lines that make up so large a part of the metrical poetry in English, we will turn, in our next chapter, to filling out our scansions with the offbeats.

PERFORMANCES, WITH COMMENTARY

Here are our performances of the second part of our first example.

```
We'll talk about rhythm –
      B            B
      B      B     B
We'll talk about beat.
      B            B
      B      B     B
```

And here is how we would do the final verses of Frost's "Stopping by Woods."

```
He gives his harness bells a shake
   B         B       B        B
To ask if there is some mistake.                    10
   B        B/b     B       B
The only other sound's the sweep
   B    B/b    B            B
Of easy wind and downy flake.
   B    B       B      B
```

```
The woods are lovely, dark and deep,
    B        B       B        B
But I have promises to keep,
    B       B   b       B
And miles to go before I sleep,
    B       B   B/b      B
And miles to go before I sleep.            15
    B       B   B/b      B
```

Note that in the above performance we've brought out the beats prominently; the only clearly unemphasized syllable that carries a beat is the third syllable in "promises." (This is a syllable that can't be given emphasis without sounding forced, and a more "spoken" performance will still allow the syllable to be experienced as a beat.) But perhaps your performance was somewhat less metrically emphatic, and so you marked some of our **B**'s as **b**'s. We've added "/**b**" after those **B**'s that could just as well have been **b**'s. You will decide for yourself how the two performances differ, though for us a strongly emphasized "before" in the last two lines suggests an energetic moving toward the future, whereas an unemphasized "before" suggests a tired longing for rest.

FURTHER PRACTICE

In the "Further Practice" section of Chapter 1, we considered choral readings, walkings, and tappings of poems by Mary Sidney, William Blake, and Emma Lazarus, along with several lines by William Wordsworth. Further consideration of these verses may be useful here, with the beat symbols instead of STEP or TAP. We have just noted in our discussion of Robert Frost's poem that differing performances will result in some people emphasizing a word that carries the beat while others will not give the same word any particular emphasis (though it will still carry a beat). So here we may review the possible choices between **B** and **b** in the "step-or-tap" poems and briefly comment on different meanings that can arise from the choice one makes.

This is the way we'd do the beats for the poem by Mary Sidney. Instead of using **B/b** to show that a beat may or may not be emphasized, as with the Frost poem, we'll show our alternative performances on separate lines.

```
Lord, on thee my trust is grounded:
 B       B      B         B
Leave me not with shame confounded;
 B       B          B        B
             b
   But in justice bring me aid.
    B    B        B     B
    b              b
Let thine ear to me be bended;
 B     B      B    B
                   b
Let my life, from death defended,          5
 B    B           B     B
   Be by thee in safety stayed.
    B    B     B      B
```

How do the two proposed readings of the second line (with or without emphasis on "not") differ? Here's what we'd say: when the "not" is emphasized, the plea "Leave me not" seems very strong: "Don't leave me, Lord, because I am bewildered and confused by shame." When there is no particular emphasis on "not," the meaning shifts to emphasize the "shame" of the speaker: "Don't abandon me to being so shameful a person."

Small **b**'s instead of large **B**'s in the third line make the performance less insistently metrical; consequently, the principal words for those things the speaker is pleading for – "justice" and "aid" – are given greater prominence. It would be possible to debate the emphasis, or lack of it, on "bring"; however, we would argue for not emphasizing the line's first word, "but," although of course it carries the beat.

The third alternative performance that we've proposed is in line four, where a lack of emphasis on "me" suggests the speaker's humility, particularly when contrasted with the strongly emphasized "thee" in the last line.

Finally, the absence of alternative performances in the last two lines, at least as we hear them, allows the eight emphasized beats to express the strength of the poet's convictions.

Of course, you may prefer still other alternative performances, such as having unemphasized **b**'s at the start of the concluding lines. If so, how would you say those performances alter, even slightly, the meanings that the lines convey?

Here is Blake's "The Lily," with our sense of the beats indicated:

```
The modest Rose puts forth a thorn:
    B       B         B         B
The humble Sheep, a threatening horn:
    B       B           B       B
While the Lily white, shall in Love delight,
        B      B                B     B
Nor a thorn nor a threat stain her beauty bright.
    B            B                 B       B
```

This seems straightforward enough to us, and we'd bet that a choral reading would arrive at this disposition of beats. But looking (and listening) carefully, one discovers that if one isolates the third line and considers it without its larger context, an alternative performance suggests itself:

```
While the Lily white, shall in Love delight,
    B       B     B      B     B     B
```

A line with six beats. Do we have a situation, then, where Blake shifts from four- to six-beat lines? Perhaps this seems like a real possibility; but for us to take it seriously, we would most likely have to find six beats in the final line as well. Will that work?

```
Nor a thorn nor a threat stain her beauty bright.
    B       B         B
```

There's the problem. We might be able to wrench the line into six beats, but feeling a beat on "a" – the first possibility we'd try – raises real doubts. So the four-beat "committee" reading deserves to prevail.

Here is where the beats come in our preferred performance of "The New Colossus" by Emma Lazarus. Determine for yourself where you might place beats differently, or where your kinds of beats – emphasized or not emphasized – might differ from ours. Can you see (or hear) why we would do it our way? Can you explain why you would do it another way, and what differences of meaning your performance would suggest?

```
Not like the brazen giant of Greek fame,
 B               B     B        B     B

With conquering limbs astride from land to land;
      B          B       B          B       B

Here at our sea-washed, sunset gates shall stand
 B         B            B      B           B

A mighty woman with a torch, whose flame
  B     B     b      B           B

Is the imprisoned lightning, and her name          5
b        B        B          b      B

Mother of Exiles. From her beacon-hand
 B      B         b      B     B

Glows world-wide welcome; her mild eyes command
      B          B            B   B      B

The air-bridged harbor that twin cities frame.
     B          B         B   B      B

"Keep, ancient lands, your storied pomp!" cries she
 B         B           B       B              B

With silent lips. "Give me your tired, your poor,  10
      B     B      B            B          B

Your huddled masses, yearning to breathe free,
      B       B       B           B      B

The wretched refuse of your teeming shore.
        B       B    b      B       B

Send these, the homeless, tempest-tossed to me,
      B         B          B       B       B

I lift my lamp beside the golden door!"
   B    B    B      B      B
```

And here, in Wordsworth's lines about avoiding ridicule, our steps are replaced by one or the other of the two kinds of beats, **B** or **b**.

```
To give and take a greeting that might save
   B       B        B           b         B
My name from piteous rumours, such as wait
   B        B        B          b       B
On men suspected to be crazed in brain.
   B     B       b     B         B
```

The various possibilities in these poems and lines for the offbeats – which according to our rule come between the beats – will be discussed in the "Further Practice" section of the next chapter.

OFFBEATS   3
o, O, -o-, [o], ô

Rhythm in English poetry is realized by the alternation of beats and offbeats. This is the principle we first proposed in our Introduction. And in Chapter 2 we showed how the scansion indicates the beats with **B**'s in their three varieties – **B**, **b**, and **[B]**. So you have already learned the first part of the system. And perhaps you have become more aware than ever before of those pleasing rhythms in metrical lines that readers take from the printed page and perform either aloud or in their own "inner ears." For the second part of the system, the offbeats, there is a larger variety of possibilities; we'll begin looking at and listening to them now.

We know, from our rule, that the offbeats will come between the beats. And in the heading of this chapter you will see the symbols for the five different sorts of offbeat that we will encounter most frequently in metrical verse.

The easiest way to become familiar with the different **o**'s is to listen to them in use. So we'll start with our First Poem. Here's where we found the **B**'s in our three performances of the poem's first line:

```
      We won't talk of stress,
         B                B

or    We won't talk of stress,
         B       B        B

or    We won't talk of stress,
            B    B        B
```

Where are the offbeats? Easy – between the beats. So they're marked this way:

```
       We won't talk of stress,
         o  B          -o-      B

or     We won't talk of stress,
         B  o      B   o      B

or     We won't talk of stress,
         o  B   ô B   o      B
```

In this example you can find three of the most common kinds of offbeat:

In our two-beat performance, we have a **double offbeat** (-o-), where two words, "talk of," are hurried over and are *together* felt as an offbeat.

In the first of our three-beat performances, there is an entirely regular alternation of beats and offbeats, so **single offbeat (o)** symbols are used to indicate it.

In the second of the three-beat performances, we have the **implied offbeat (ô)**, an offbeat which occurs where there is no word or part of a word that occupies the space between two beats (and where no punctuation or other obvious break creates a distinct pause). We sense this necessary pause because an energetic performance of the words **"won't talk"** creates an eddy in the smooth flow of the line. This tendency to sense a pause or hesitation, though not an actual moment of silence, between strongly stressed syllables is a feature of the way English is spoken, a feature which metrical verse makes use of – though it always produces a disruption in the regular alternations of the rhythm. (Users of word processing programs will find several easy ways of keyboarding the implied offbeat symbol, ô, in the list of scansion symbols, page 149.)

Let's scan our second line, in its three performances:

```
       We won't talk of feet.
         o  B          -o-      B

or     We won't talk of feet.
         B  o      B   o      B

or     We won't talk of feet.
         o  B   ô B   o      B
```

And now let's complete the scansion of our final lines – which have only two possibilities of performance (because we don't want to mispronounce "about"). Notice that our implied offbeat now is experienced between the vigorously emphasized "a**bout**" and the equally emphasized syllables "**rhyth**-" and "**beat**":

Two-beat version:

```
We'll talk about rhythm —
  o    B   -o-    B  o
We'll talk about beat.
  o    B   -o-    B
```

Three-beat version:

```
We'll talk about rhythm —
  o    B  o B ô B  o
We'll talk about beat.
  o    B  o B ô B
```

For those occasional instances where we encounter double offbeats with certain *emphasized* syllables, the -o- symbol can be varied. If your performance gives an emphasis to the first syllable of the double offbeat, this symbol will indicate it: =**o**-. If the second syllable of the double offbeat is emphasized, this symbol is used: -**o**=. In *exceedingly* rare circumstances both offbeat syllables can be emphasized: =**o**=. (This would represent a very energy-charged performance indeed.) Here are examples, in two-beat lines:

```
With song in the street,
We'll say, "Hear the beat,"
  o    B       =o-    B

Or being discreet,
We'll murmur, "Nice beat."
  o    B   -o=     B

If noises compete,
We'll shout, "Far-out beat!"
  o     B        =o=    B
```

In this context of two-beat lines, perhaps one will suppress a bit of the natural emphasis on "Hear," "Nice," and both parts of "Far-out"; what our = sign indicates is just this tension between a word that demands a certain degree of emphasis and a meter that demands – at this point – very little.

The two opening lines of our second poem are scanned in the following way, by adding the offbeats between the *pronounced* beats we noted in Chapter 2. You'll see just how the rhythms of the lines as we heard them have been represented very fully by our **B**'s and our three different kinds of **o**.

```
        Hickory dickory dock,
         B   -o-  B  -o-  B

        The verse ticks like a clock.
          o  B    o    B  o  B

or      The verse ticks like a clock.
          o  B   ô B        -o-  B
```

Here there are regular offbeats, double offbeats, and an implied offbeat (between the strongly emphasized words "verse" and "ticks" in the last example). Notice that the first of the two alternative ways of performing the second line means treating the word "ticks" as having no more emphasis than words like "the" or "a": this only happens if we're *chanting* the verse, which means exaggerating the beat–offbeat pattern. As we said earlier, the second alternative is closer to the way someone would speak this sentence normally.

Let's complete our scansion of the pronounced syllables in our second poem by adding the offbeats:

```
            But when the clock unwinds,
              o   B   o   B   o B

            Its mechanism grinds,
             o   B   o b o   B

            And it stops.
              -o-     B

or perhaps  And it stops.
            B   o   B
```

How would you read the unwinding-clock line if it went like this?

```
But when the clock winds down
```

If we say the line in the rhythm established by the previous lines, we will experience emphases not on two of the line's final words, like "**clock** un**winds**," but on three of them: "**clock winds down**." Rather than sensing three beats in a row, though, we'll feel the two beats where we expect them with an offbeat in between. For this situation, we have another type of offbeat, the **emphasized offbeat**, whose symbol is a capital **O**:

```
But when the clock winds down
 o    B    o    B    O    B
```

Emphasized offbeats will be turning up in many of the lines we'll be encountering, making their contribution to the spoken quality and energy of the poems in which they occur.

It may seem to you that we're accumulating quite a number of symbols. But one soon becomes familiar with their use; and when that happens, problems vanish and we discover that we are responding fully to the pleasures of rhythm that centuries of poets writing metrically in earlier periods and our own have prepared for us.

Let's now complete the scansion of the first two stanzas of "Stopping by Woods on a Snowy Evening," showing Frost's use of some of the different kinds of beat and offbeat. Note that just as the scene is a calm and "easy" one, the scansion is on the whole very regular – the **B**'s and **o**'s follow each other with a confident orderliness. Our own preferred performance – perhaps not yours – for line three is given here; note how the "beat, double offbeat, beat" pattern works, and listen carefully to how it sounds:

```
Whose woods these are I think I know.
  o    B     o   b  o   B  o   B
His house is in the village though;
  o    B    o  b   o  B  o     B
He will not see me stopping here
 B    -o-   B   o   B  o    B
To watch his woods fill up with snow.
  o   B    o   B    o  B   o     B
```

```
My little horse must think it queer          5
 o  B   o  B     o    B  o  B
To stop without a farmhouse near
 o  B  o  B  o  B  o    B
Between the woods and frozen lake
 o  B    o  B    o   B o  B
The darkest evening of the year.
   o  B  o  B   o   b    o  B
```

We gave our reasons in Chapter 2 for preferring an emphasis on "He" in the third line. It will become clear, as we encounter more instances, that the "beat, double offbeat, beat" pattern is a very common one for the beginnings of lines in innumerable poems.

You may remember that also in Chapter 2, when discussing the beats in line six, we said that later "we will see how beat scansion can show nearly equal emphasis on 'farm' and 'house.'" Let's look at that now, because it will give us another chance to use our symbol for an emphasized offbeat. Though the two parts of "farmhouse" probably aren't given as much emphasis as, say, the two parts of the common slang phrase "far-out," you might wish to emphasize the "house" part in your own performance and mark it accordingly. So here's how it would look, using the symbol **O**:

```
To stop without a farmhouse near
 o  B  o  B  o  B  O    B
```

We've been saying right along that even small differences in performance will create differences in meaning; if in this line "house" were emphasized along with "farm," the entire absence of dwellings, of other people, might be brought out more strongly. Perhaps, too, we would be reminded of the other house in the poem, the house of the owner of the woods; then our sense of the solitariness of the person who stops by woods on a snowy evening would be enhanced.

If you scanned the beats in the last two stanzas of Frost's poem, as suggested in Chapter 2, you may want to complete your scansion now by including the offbeats. That will be easy, because all of the offbeats are single ones coming regularly between the **B**'s and **b**'s, just where one would expect them.

The first performance of our five-beat poem about Elizabeth Barrett Browning would have its offbeats indicated in this way:

```
Elizabeth Barrett Browning counted ways
o B -o-   B o    B o   B   o   B
She loved her poet-husband. We can hear
  o B   o  Bo  B o    B  o  B
The ways she counted beats, so that her praise
  o B   o B  o  B    o  B   o   B
Would come as music to our inner ear.
  o    B  o  B o   bo   B o B
```

But what offbeats do we find in the third line's alternative performance, where the line's third and fourth beats fall on the words "beats" and "so"? There are regular single and double offbeats, and there is also our final "new" one, the **virtual offbeat [o]**:

```
The ways she counted beats, so that her praise
  o B    o B  o  B [o] B   -o-    B
```

Here the symbol for the virtual offbeat lets us record our performance of a line where an obvious break, coinciding with the comma but not caused by it, creates a distinct pause.

Now, adding the offbeats to the stanza from the Herrick poem in the previous chapter, we can complete our overview of the essentials of beat scansion:

```
Gather ye rosebuds while ye may,
 B  -o-  B  o    B   o B
Old time is still a-flying;
O   B  o   B  o Bo   [B]
And this same flower that smiles today
 o   B  O   B    o   B   o B
Tomorrow will be dying.
 o B  o   b   o Bo   [B]
```

If you normally pronounce the word "flower" with two syllables, you will probably scan the third line as follows:

```
And this same flower that smiles today
o      B  O  B  -o-     B    o B
```

It's very likely that Herrick pronounced the word – at least in this poem – as one syllable, however; like many poets who control the number of syllables in their lines, he uses double offbeats only in certain circumstances (more on this later). Notice too the upper-case **O**'s in our scansion: they imply a certain degree of emphasis on "Old" and "same," an emphasis that we think the sense deserves. You may think otherwise – for instance, that "Old" is just a conventional adjective for "time" that needn't get any more stress than, say, "The" would at this point. In this case, you would write a lower-case **o** in your scansion.

This single Herrick stanza, then, uses our two principal beats, **B** and **b**, and the virtual beat [**B**] – here following the spoken "-ing" offbeats of "flying" and "dying." (For those three-beat lines which do not end with a spoken offbeat, the virtual beat symbol [**B**] represents – in accordance with our metrical rule – both the beat and the necessary pause, or offbeat, which precedes it.) The example also uses three of the five common offbeats: **o, O,** and **-o-**.

So with just our three kinds of beat (**B, b,** and [**B**]) and five kinds of offbeat (**o, O, -o-, ô,** and [**o**]), revealing scansions of any metrical poems the reader–performer of poetry may encounter can be completed: we have covered the basics. In our next chapter we will put these basics to work with new poems. There we will become ever more aware of the artistry and metrical sensitivity of many of the best-loved writers of poetry in English, and of how this metrical sensitivity contributes to their poems' meanings and emotional subtleties.

FURTHER PRACTICE

Here are completed scansions of the poems to which beats were added at the end of Chapter 2. These are our preferred scansions. What alternatives can you suggest? How do they change, even subtly, a line's meaning, or its tone?

You may find that occasionally you feel there is an unstressed syllable not marked in the scansion: would you, for instance, pronounce "threatening" and "conquering" as two or three syllables? Both are common pronunciations. We've already seen a different kind of example in "flower" – one or two syllables? Although these different pronunciations mean different scansions, they don't cause any significant disruption to the flow of the rhythm – partly because the additional syllable is always a very weak one (you may even be unsure as to whether you do hear it as a separate syllable), and partly because single and double offbeats play a very similar role in the alternating rhythm of English meter.

First, the poem by Mary Sidney (p. 30):

```
Lord, on thee my trust is grounded:
 B   o   B   o   B   o   B   o

Leave me not with shame confounded;
 B    o  b  o   B    o  B   o

   But in justice bring me aid.
    b  o  B   o    b   o B

Let thine ear to me be bended;
 B   o   B   o  b  o B   o

Let my life, from death defended,              5
 B  o  B    o   B    o B  o

   Be by thee in safety stayed.
    B  o  B  o   B    o   B
```

Here is our performance of Blake's "The Lily" (p. 31). You will note that we hear an emphasis on the word "stain" in the final line; as it is part of a double offbeat, the **=o-** variation of the double-offbeat symbol is used.

```
The modest Rose puts forth a thorn:
  o  B o    B    o    B    o  B
The humble Sheep, a threatening horn:
  o  B   o   B    o    B    o   B
While the Lily white, shall in Love delight,
   -o-    B o  B        -o-   B   o B
Nor a thorn nor a threat stain her beauty bright.
 -o-   B    -o-    B      =o-   B  o  B
```

What meaning, by the way, do you take from this enigmatic little poem, which we've now encountered for a third time? Is the Lily, delighting in Love, an emblem of virtue and purity as opposed to the Rose and Sheep, with their more complex, partly hurtful double natures? Or is the Lily simply less overt in acknowledging her complexity?

It isn't easy to choose. That word "while" in line 3 can mean both "even though" (a contrast) and "at the same time that" (a similarity). Then too, the unexpected emphasis on the word "stain" in the final double offbeat seems odd when the expected emphases would be on "beauty" and "bright" alone. (Compare Blake's line with this: "Nor a thorn nor a threat in her beauty bright.") What do you think? Is Blake here asking us to consider questions whose answers must be decided by each of us individually?

Our completed scansion of "The New Colossus" (p. 32) would be as follows (the symbols under line 5 indicate a disagreement: one of us gives "Is" some emphasis, the other doesn't). Note again, in line 9, the instance of a double offbeat with one of its syllables emphasized. Do you feel that this performance of the line – a necessary one, we would say – thus adds energy to what the statue, the Mother of Exiles, announces?

```
Not like the brazen giant of Greek fame,
 B      -o-     B o  B -o-   B  ô B
With conquering limbs astride from land to land;
 o    B     o    B    o    B    o   B   o   B
Here at our sea-washed, sunset gates shall stand
 B     -o-    B   O       B  o  B    o    B
```

```
A mighty woman with a torch, whose flame
o  B   o  B  o   b   o  B       o   B

Is the imprisoned lightning, and her name        5
o   b o   B    o   B    o   b   o  B
b    -o-    B

Mother of Exiles. From her beacon-hand
 B   -o-  B o       b  o   B o   B

Glows world-wide welcome; her mild eyes command
 O    B    O    B     -o-    B  ôB   o  B

The air-bridged harbor that twin cities frame.
 o  B    O     B    -o-     B ô B o    B

"Keep, ancient lands, your storied pomp!" cries she
 B    =o-     B    o    B o   B       o    B

With silent lips. "Give me your tired, your poor,  10
 o   B o   B  [o] B   -o-   B    o   B

Your huddled masses, yearning to breathe free,
 o   B    o   B  o    B     -o-   B  ô B

The wretched refuse of your teeming shore.
 o   B   o   B o   b  o   B  o    B

Send these, the homeless, tempest-tossed to me,
 O    B    o  B   o   B  o   B    o B

I lift my lamp beside the golden door!"
o  B   o  B    o B    o  B o   B
```

We find particularly moving the four emphasized words at the beginning of line 7, "Glows world-wide welcome" (made even more prominent by the alliteration of "world-wide welcome").

Finally, the Wordsworth lines (p. 33), where his dog's warning of approaching people permits the poet

```
To give and take a greeting that might save
 o  B   o   B   o  B o   b   o    B

My name from piteous rumours, such as wait
 o  B    o  B o    B o    b   o   B

On men suspected to be crazed in brain.
 o  B   o B o  b  o  B   o   B
```

Notice that with the completion of the scansion for the first line, an alternative scansion suggests itself:

```
To give and take a greeting that might save
 o  B   o   B   o  B   -o-    B  ô B
```

This seems to us perhaps the more interesting performance, because the stronger emphasis on "might" in "might save" hints that the poet is expressing, with this word, his uncertainty that he will ever escape being thought of as crazy by the practical people in his neighborhood.

SCANNING POEMS 4

In this chapter we will apply the principles of scansion that we have been discussing to a variety of poems, or excerpts from poems. And, as in earlier chapters, we will work with poems of varying line lengths. Because shorter-line-length poems are the most evidently rhythmical ones, we will begin with several of them.

SHORTER-LINE-LENGTH POEMS

A poem many have loved for almost two hundred years is "I Wandered Lonely as a Cloud," written by William Wordsworth in 1804 when he was about thirty-four years old. The poet, out on a walk, suddenly comes across a lake's edge bordered by thousands of daffodils; the memory of this wonderful sight stays with him and gives him pleasure in thoughtful moments later in life.

Let's begin, as usual, by performing the four stanzas of the poem aloud:

```
I wandered lonely as a cloud
That floats on high o'er vales and hills,
When all at once I saw a crowd,
A host, of golden daffodils;
Beside the lake, beneath the trees,                    5
Fluttering and dancing in the breeze.

Continuous as the stars that shine
And twinkle on the milky way,
```

```
They stretched in never-ending line
Along the margin of a bay:                              10
Ten thousand saw I at a glance,
Tossing their heads in sprightly dance.

The waves beside them danced; but they
Outdid the sparkling waves in glee;
A poet could not but be gay,                            15
In such a jocund company;
I gazed — and gazed — but little thought
What wealth the show to me had brought:

For oft, when on my couch I lie
In vacant or in pensive mood,                           20
They flash upon that inward eye
Which is the bliss of solitude;
And then my heart with pleasure fills,
And dances with the daffodils.
```

Like Frost for "Stopping by Woods," Wordsworth has chosen for this meditative poem a very even meter. In performances of the first four lines, particularly, the alternation of **B**'s and **o**'s will probably be quite regular; even the lack of emphasis on the "as" in the first line adds to a sense of relaxed ease. Here is our performance of these lines – perhaps very close to yours:

```
I wandered lonely as a cloud
o  B  o    B  o b o    B
That floats on high o'er vales and hills,
  o  B    o  B  o    B    o    B
When all at once I saw a crowd,
  o  B   o B    o B o   B
A host, of golden daffodils;
o  B   o  B  o   B  o b
```

It's possible that you had **B**'s where we had **b**'s; this would give a bit more emphasis to the meter, but it perhaps makes the poem too sing-song, as if Wordsworth were choosing his words for their rhythm rather than their meaning. All, however, are likely to notice that the last line of the stanza changes the rhythm a bit – with very expressive results. Let's perform the final two lines of the stanza and identify where their beats and offbeats are heard:

```
Beside the lake, beneath the trees,
Fluttering and dancing in the breeze.
```

Here is our performance:

```
Beside the lake, beneath the trees,
 o B    o B    o B     o  B

Fluttering and dancing in the breeze.
  B      -o-   B  o  b  o  B
```

Certainly the first syllable in the last line, "Flut-," carries the beat. And it's likely that Wordsworth pronounced the word "fluttering" as "flut-ring" – two syllables instead of the three some may hear. So we've marked this line with a double offbeat. If you wish to say, no, "ter-ing and" makes up a triple offbeat, that's fine too, and there is a sign for your performance: the rarely-encountered triple offbeat is represented in this way: ~o~. (As with "threatening" and "conquering," encountered in the Blake and Lazarus poems, the middle syllable of "fluttering," when the word is pronounced with three syllables, is very weak, and so doesn't make a significant difference to the rhythm.) This would be the scansion for the triple-offbeat performance of the line:

```
Fluttering and dancing in the breeze.
  B      ~o~   B  o  b  o  B
```

Whichever performance is yours, it is the effect of this slight change in rhythm from what was encountered in all of the earlier lines that is important. What do you experience when Wordsworth makes this unexpected shift? Of course he could have written something absolutely regular, like this:

```
Alive and dancing in the breeze.
 o B   o   B  o  b  o  B
```

What, though, is the difference in the feel of the words "alive" and "fluttering"? Both are words that suggest animation, but why is "fluttering" the better choice rhythmically?

This question is one which every performer will have to answer for himself or herself, but you've probably guessed that our answer is that just like the daffodils, the word "fluttering" flutters – it takes longer to say, the tongue has to flutter a bit just to pronounce the word, and the change of rhythm brings its own sense of surprise to the scene. In the word itself, then, there is a kind of jittery animation which helps convey the visual image better than a more regularly metrical word would have done.

And having given that extra degree of energy to the last line of his first stanza, Wordsworth does the same thing at the beginning of the second stanza. The double offbeat in "Continuous as the stars that shine" lengthens the time it takes to pronounce the first part of the line, and so enhances the sense of an almost eternal beauty in the scene that the poet is observing. Imagine the difference between Wordsworth's line as it is and something a lesser poet might have written, like "As lovely as the stars that shine" – not only a lesser idea, but a duller metrical performance.

But let's perform the second stanza as a whole, now, and listen particularly for the slight differences from the expected pattern of large **B**'s and small **o**'s in this stanza's two final lines.

```
Continuous as the stars that shine
  o  B -o- b   o  B    o    B

And twinkle on the milky way,
  o     B   o b   o  B  o B

They stretched in never-ending line
   o     B      o   B o B  o    B

Along the margin of a bay:                        10
 o B    o  B  o b  o B

Ten thousand saw I at a glance,
  O    B  o    B  o b o   B

Tossing their heads in sprightly dance.
  B    -o-     B    o      B   o B
```

If your performance was like ours, you gave the "ten" in "Ten thousand" the extra energy that turned the **o** into an **O** and added to the sense of wonder and astonishment that the poet seems to be feeling. And "Tossing" repeats the trick of "Fluttering" (though without the flicker of an extra unstressed syllable), giving us a metrical sense of the continued animation of the flowers.

But check back, now; note that in all of Wordsworth's lines we have sensed and marked four beats – **B**'s and **b**'s. Between every beat has appeared, according to the rule for meter in English, an offbeat of one kind or another – here, **o**, **O**, and -**o**- (or perhaps in line six, ~**o**~). By marking these beats and offbeats we have been able to show by meaningful symbols where our own physical energies have contributed to our experience of Wordsworth's physical delight in a memorable display of natural beauty.

How does your scansion of the final stanzas, where the after-effects of the experience are described, compare with ours?

```
The waves beside them danced; but they
  o B     o B      o  B      o   B

Outdid the sparkling waves in glee;
O  B   o   B    o   B    o   B

A poet could not but be gay,                    15
o  Bo    B    o   b   o B

In such a jocund company;
o  B   o  B o     B   o b

I gazed — and gazed — but little thought
o B      o    B       o   B  o   B

What wealth the show to me had brought:
  O    B       o   B   o B o    B


For oft, when on my couch I lie
  o  B     o  b   o  B    o B

In vacant or in pensive mood,                   20
o  B o   b  o   B    o    B

They flash upon that inward eye
  o   B    o b    o   B o   B
```

```
Which is the bliss of solitude;
  o    b    o    B    o    B o b
And then my heart with pleasure fills,
o     B   o  B     o      B  o   B
And dances with the daffodils.
o     B   o   b     o  B  o b
```

In our second chapter we began discussion of the "ballad stanza," a very popular verse form from early times which in its most usual form alternates lines of four beats with lines of three spoken beats (though felt as four-beat lines with an additional virtual beat). As we've mentioned, another name for this stanza – which is by no means confined to traditional ballads – is "common meter" (or "common measure"). Common meter, used in many hymns, is the basis for a large number of poems by Emily Dickinson (1830–86), who spent her adulthood living reclusively in Amherst, Massachusetts, who published only seven poems during her lifetime but left behind nearly 1,800, and who is now widely regarded as one of America's finest and most original poets. To look at, perform, and scan one of her poems is to discover how skillfully she uses a regular meter, with some occasional rhythmic variations, to enhance the meanings and emotional effects of her poetry.

Dickinson's poems are known by their opening words, and here is "I Died for Beauty," a poem with an unusual setting – two people are speaking to one another while in their graves.

```
I died for Beauty – but was scarce
Adjusted in the Tomb
When One who died for Truth, was lain
In an adjoining Room –

He questioned softly "Why I failed"?                 5
"For Beauty", I replied –
"And I – for Truth – Themself are One –
We Brethren, are", He said –

And so, as Kinsmen, met a Night –
We talked between the Rooms –                        10
Until the Moss had reached our lips –
And covered up – our names –
```

In the poem you will notice that Dickinson uses a device often used by poets to keep their meter regular: instead of saying "We are Brethren," she reverses this natural word order so that the beats will come where she wants them – "We Brethren, are." (Most contemporary poets try to avoid this device, called "inversion," because readers these days tend to prefer a more usual word order.) Also, Dickinson employs a word from medieval times, "anight," instead of saying "at night." Perhaps she does this because "a Night," which has an unemphatic "a" followed by a definitely emphasized "Night," helps create a regular, calm-sounding line that seems to suit the relaxed tone of the deathly conversation. "Met at night," with its three prominent "t" sounds, would sound harsher.

Here is the performance we would give this remarkable poem – including the virtual beats. How closely does it match yours? If your performance has differences, what nuances of meaning are changed by the changed performance?

```
I died for Beauty — but was scarce
o B   o B   o  b   o    B

Adjusted in the Tomb
o B o b   o B   [B]

When One who died for Truth, was lain
  o B    o B   o   B   o  B

In an adjoining Room —
o b o B o   B    [B]

He questioned softly "Why I failed"?          5
 o  B  o    B  o   B o B

"For Beauty", I replied —
  o  B   o b o B   [B]

"And I — for Truth — Themself are One —
 o  B   o  B      o B o   B

We Brethren, are", He said —
O   B   o  b    o B   [B]

And so, as Kinsmen, met a Night —
o   B o  B    o   B o B
```

```
We talked between the Rooms —                          10
  o  B      o  B      o  B      [B]
Until the Moss had reached our lips —
  o  B  o  B   o  B      o   B
And covered up — our names —
  o    B o   b   o   B      [B]
```

If you have come across some of her poems before, you will be aware that Emily Dickinson often uses dashes instead of more conventional punctuation. Perhaps this is simply to suggest a slight moment of reflection before thought moves on, or to control the pacing of a line. We can, if we wish, observe the dashes as brief silences in our performances, but it must be recognized that such dramatic breaks have *no effect whatever* on the underlying meter. The **B**'s and **o**'s progress in their normal ways, with their normal variations, in no way changed by these marks. The same is true for punctuation generally. Commas, semicolons, and other marks are never, *by them-selves*, elements that determine the metricality of a line. As we have already observed, virtual or implied offbeats – particularly implied offbeats, where there is no sense of a break in the rhythm – may be felt where there is no punctuation at all.

The ballad stanza Dickinson uses in "I Died for Beauty" is the standard one, with four-beat and three-beat lines alternating without variation. (A shorthand way of identifying this stanza is to say it is a 4.3.4.3 stanza.) Historically, though, there have been ballads written in different arrangements of four- and three-beat lines, and one that occurs with some frequency is the three-beat, three-beat, four-beat, three-beat (or 3.3.4.3) stanza. Here is an example by the great English novelist and perhaps even greater poet, Thomas Hardy, who was born in 1840 and became a church architect before turning definitively to writing. In this poem, "I Look into My Glass," published in his first collection when he was fifty-eight and sensing the approach of death (though he lived another thirty years and published seven more books of verse!), the speaker looks into a mirror and meditates on the difference between what he sees and how he feels. Try performing it aloud. Do you sense that the longer four-beat lines in each stanza have a different feel than the three-beat lines?

```
I look into my glass,
And view my wasting skin,
And say, "Would God it came to pass
My heart had shrunk as thin!"

For then, I, undistressed                              5
By hearts grown cold to me,
Could lonely wait my endless rest
With equanimity.

But Time, to make me grieve,
Part steals, lets part abide;                         10
And shakes this fragile frame at eve
With throbbings of noontide.
```

The poem is quite regular, and seems to offer only a few moments
of possible indecision about its scansion. But let's look at the way
the stanzas might be marked, because some emphases and rhyth-
mical movements will thus be made clearer and, as a result, more
meaningful.

```
I look into my glass,
o  B   o  b  o   B    [B]

And view my wasting skin,
o   B   o B  o    B   [B]

And say, "Would God it came to pass
o   B    O    B o  B   o B

My heart had shrunk as thin!"
 o  B    o     B   o   B   [B]


For then, I, undistressed                             5
 o   B  O B o   B    [B]

By hearts grown cold to me,
 o B      O    B   o B [B]

Could lonely wait my endless rest
 o    B  o B   oB  o    B

With equanimity.
 o   B o  B o b  [B]
```

```
But Time, to make me grieve,
 o  B    o B   o  B     [B]

Part steals, lets part abide;                          10
 O    B     o    B   o B    [B]

And shakes this fragile frame at eve
 o     B     o    B  o    B   o B

With throbbings of noontide.
 o      B      -o-  B  ôB    [B]
```

One might remark that because the two opening lines in every stanza have three beats followed by the virtual beat, their shortness and abruptness are emphasized: the statements that they make seem more matter-of-fact than laden with emotion. In the first stanza the poet notes his aged appearance; in the second, he imagines being undistressed by lack of love; in the third, he claims that Time steals his body but not his heart, calling each merely a "part" of himself. Yet when in each stanza the four-beat line is encountered, a different, more intensely emotional mood is created which carries through to the end of its stanza. The first stanza's four-beat line begins voicing the poet's urgent wish that God had shrunk his heart as well as his skin; the longer line of stanza two suggests the length of his lonely wait for death's endless rest; and in the final stanza's four-beat line the aging body shakes with the desires of youth. Without virtual beats or punctuation at their ends, these lines lead with poignant smoothness into the three-beat lines that conclude each stanza. Finally, beats on each syllable of "noontide" join with the final virtual beat to bring the poem to a grimly emphatic close.

Would Hardy's poem have created a different effect if he had used the more common 4.3.4.3 ballad stanza pattern? One can imagine four-beat lines at the beginning of the stanzas, such as "I look again into my glass," and "For then, I, being undistressed," and "But Time, resolved to make me grieve." Try out these substitute lines for yourself; do you sense the difference? It seems to us that the tensions created by Hardy's shorter lines would be relaxed, and the poem would become less anguished.

A final example of a poem using three- and four-beat lines returns us for a moment to Emily Dickinson. Here is an unusual transformation

of the ballad stanza, where a four-beat line comes first in each
of the two stanzas, to be followed by three-beat lines. Perhaps it
is the opening line of each stanza that seems particularly emo-
tional, while the lines that follow explain more coolly the reasons
for the emotion. What do you think? Here is the poem, with a likely
scansion.

```
I like a look of Agony,
o  B    o  B    o   B o b
Because I know it's true —
 o  B    o    B  o       B   [B]
Men do not sham Convulsion,
 B   -o-    B    o B   o   [B]
Nor simulate, a Throe —
 o    B o b    o    B    [B]

The Eyes glaze once — and that is Death —          5
  o B       O    B      o     B o  B
Impossible to feign
o  B  o  b  o  B    [B]
The Beads upon the Forehead
  o  B    o B    o  B   o   [B]
By homely Anguish strung.
  o  B   o B  o       B    [B]
```

Before moving on to longer line-length poems, it may be useful here
to consider three ballad stanzas from yet another Wordsworth poem,
"Strange Fits of Passion Have I Known," in which the alternation
of eight- and six-syllable lines is carefully controlled. In short space
they further demonstrate and contrast the use of virtual and implied
offbeats, and of double offbeats.

   You may have noticed that when we encounter one of these
"offbeats without the spoken syllable" there is usually a double
offbeat nearby, as at the conclusion of Hardy's "I Look into My
Glass," where the poet speaks of "**throbb**ings of **noon-tide**." In
stricter kinds of metrical verse this is an extremely common event, as
though the absence of the spoken offbeat is compensated for by an
"extra" spoken syllable elsewhere in the line. And the reverse is true,

too. In syllable-controlled verse there will seldom be a double offbeat unless there is an implied or virtual offbeat nearby.

Here are the two stanzas from "Strange Fits of Passion" which contrast the two kinds of "unpronounced" offbeats – each of which has its accompanying double offbeat. First we have the *implied offbeat*, then the *virtual offbeat*:

```
Upon the moon I fixed my eye,
All over the wide lea
O   B  -o-   B  ô B  [B]

With quickening pace my horse drew nigh
Those paths so dear to me.

.  .  .

My horse moved on; hoof after hoof
 o  B   O    B [o]B  -o-   B

He raised, and never stopped:
When down behind the cottage roof,
At once, the bright moon dropped.
```

When performing these examples one can experience quite vividly the difference between implied and virtual offbeats. Although there is no definite break between "wide" and "lea," the rhythm encourages the reader to slow down on the two words so that they become the *equivalent* of two beats separated by an offbeat. There is, as we said when introducing the implied offbeat in Chapter 3, an "eddy in the smooth flow of the line." Between "on" and "hoof," however, there's a distinct break in the rhythm, as if indeed there were an offbeat between them. (This doesn't mean there has to be a moment of silence in the performance, though; it's just as effective to make "on" a little longer than usual, provided the break in the rhythm is *felt*.)

As these examples show, in verse where syllable-count is strictly controlled, a double offbeat can be expected in lines containing an implied or virtual offbeat; and an implied or virtual offbeat can be expected in lines containing a double offbeat. But in one frequently encountered circumstance, a double offbeat will appear in lines which contain neither of the "unpronounced" offbeats. This happens at the beginnings of lines of verse which start with a beat followed by a double offbeat, then another beat (like Wordsworth's earlier "**Toss**ing their **heads**"). Here it's the *lack* of an expected opening offbeat which is compensated for by the double offbeat, and so the number of syllables stays the same. (This little rhythmic pattern will be discussed further in the following chapter.)

Our third "Strange Fits of Passion" stanza, then, has two lines performed with the beat, double-offbeat, beat opening. Neither of them has an additional "unpronounced" offbeat – or needs one to maintain both the rhythm and the poet's eight-six syllable count:

```
When she I loved looked every day
Fresh as a rose in June,
  B    -o- B   o   B    [B]
I to her cottage bent my way,
B  -o-   B o   B   o  B
Beneath an evening-moon.
```

In our scansions of longer-line poems there will be many instances of the patterns illustrated by lines in these three Wordsworth stanzas.

LONGER-LINE-LENGTH POEMS

Poems with four, or three, or mixed four-and-three pronounced beats make up a very large proportion of poetry written in English – and, as has been mentioned, almost all song lyrics use these four-beat meters. Even when we read poems with lines of two beats, we usually experience the meter as four-beat lines divided in half. (You will recollect how our "man from Japan/Whose limericks never would scan" had too much to say "When **friends** asked him **why**/He re**plied** with a **sigh**.") Also, poems written in much longer lines – lines of six, seven, or eight beats – usually turn out to be experienced as a combination or mixture of four-beat and "three-beat-plus-virtual-fourth-beat" lines.

The one reasonably short line that *doesn't* have a tendency to be performed with the song-like rhythms of four-beat meters is the five-beat line. In use since the late 1300s, often for poems of a serious nature but for many other kinds of poem as well, this metrical line has been a boon to poets aiming to achieve a rhythm closer to the speaking voice. The line predominates in Shakespeare's plays. Here are Macbeth and Romeo using the five-beat line in often-performed soliloquies:

```
Is this a dagger which I see before me,
o   B   o B  o    b  o B  o B   o
The handle toward my hand? Come, let me clutch thee!
  o  B   o  b    o  B [o]B    -o-   B    o

But soft, what light from yonder window breaks?
  o  B    O   B    o  B  o  B  o   B
It is the east and Juliet is the sun!
B  -o-  B   o   B o  b   o B
  o  b   o
```

Shakespeare's lines are, not surprisingly, very "spoken" sounding, but the underlying meter is there – often with many of the variations we have been discussing.

Shakespeare's plays are his most remarkable achievements, but in his collection of 154 sonnets – fourteen-line poems following a fixed metrical pattern and rhyme-scheme – he also creates a fascinating range of metrical effects in five-beat lines. The openings of three of his most famous sonnets illustrate some of the rhythmical variations the poet can achieve while still staying within the requirements of the meter. Here are our performances of these lines (which are not the only ways to read them):

```
That time of year thou mayst in me behold      (73)
  o  B  o  B    o  B   o  B  oB
Shall I compare thee to a summer's day         (18)
  B  -o-  B    o  b o B  o    B
When, in disgrace with Fortune and men's eyes  (29)
  B   -o-   B    o   B   -o-  B  ôB
```

If you say these lines aloud with these suggested performances, you will hear how the poet adapts his meters to his meanings: Sonnet 73 is a quiet lament about how a loved one must see the poet growing old, and the easy regularity of the meter suggests a calm resignation; Sonnet 18 is more lively, with a less even rhythm as the poet compares his love to a summer's day and claims that summer has deficiencies that his love does not; and Sonnet 29, full of self-accusation and "myself almost despising," begins with an anguished statement in a troubled meter. Although all the lines have their five beats, you will notice striking differences between them, particularly between the first and the last.

As an exercise in scanning an entire Shakespeare sonnet, copy out, read aloud, and then scan Sonnet 50, where the speaker is riding his horse toward a place where he ought to be glad to find rest, but where he knows he will be miserable because he has left his friend behind.

> How heavy do I journey on the way
> When what I seek, my weary travel's end,
> Doth teach that ease and that repose to say
> "Thus far the miles are measured from thy friend."
> The beast that bears me, tired with my woe,   5
> Plods dully on, to bear that weight in me,
> As if by some instinct the wretch did know
> His rider loved not speed being made from thee.
> The bloody spur cannot provoke him on
> That sometimes anger thrusts into his hide,   10
> Which heavily he answers with a groan
> More sharp to me than spurring to his side;
>   For that same groan doth put this in my mind:
>   My grief lies onward and my joy behind.

Here is our performance of the poem, with some alternatives indicated, and a discussion of our preferred readings and other possibilities – some of which you may feel give clearer expression to your own sense of the words.

```
How heavy do I journey on the way
 O  B  o  bo  B  o  b   o  B

When what I seek, my weary travel's end,
  o    B o B    o B o   B o    B
```

```
Doth teach that ease and that repose to say
 o   B     O    B    o      B    oB    o B

"Thus far the miles are measured from thy friend."
  O   B    o  B    o    B  o        b    o   B

The beast that bears me, tired with my woe,          5
  o   B      o    B     o    B o   b   o  B

Plods dully on, to bear that weight in me,
  O     B  o B    o   B    O    B   o   B

As if by some instinct the wretch did know
 o  B   o  B   ôB      -o-      B   o    B
                o     B      o

His rider lov'd not speed being made from thee.
 o   B  o  B     o    B    o     B    o    B
                            -o-

The bloody spur cannot provoke him on
 o   B  o   B   o  B    oB     o  B
             ô  B  -o-

That sometimes anger thrusts into his hide,        10
 o    B    o    B  o      B    o  b o   B
                           B   ôB -o-   B

Which heavily he answers with a groan,
 o     B  o b oB   o    b   o   B

More sharp to me than spurring to his side;
 O     B    o B   o   B    -o-   B ô B

  For that same groan doth put this in my mind:
   o    B   O    B    o    B    o  b  o B
                        B ô B  -o-   B

  My grief lies onward and my joy behind.
   o   B    o   B   o  b   o B   oB
```

We feel that the poem begins slackly, with only three prominent beats in the first line (of course there are five beats, but only **hea**vy, **jour**ney, and **way** have much emphasis). The mood is rhythmically well established here. ("Heavy," incidentally, can mean both "sadly" and "slowly," and it also implies, at least in view of what comes later, that the speaker's grief has a real weight which is slowing down the horse's progress.) For the first six lines there are no alterations of the most regular rhythmic pattern other than the occasional use of **b** and **O**. When there are moments of heightened emotion or anger, however, the lines get more emphatic before again subsiding into gloom.

Line 12, for example, is a particularly tormented one. On first reading, the following might have occurred to you as a likely alternative to the performance we've indicated:

```
More sharp to me than spurring to his side;
  O     B   o B  o  B   o    b o   B
```

That thought occurred to us. But then we looked more closely at the *meaning* of the line: the unhappy speaker is comparing the sharp pang of grief given to *him* by the horse's groan with the sharp pain his angry spurring gave to *the horse*. It then seemed to us that the line demands emphasis on both "me" and "his" to bring out this contrast strongly – and, at the same time, to produce a troubling of the line's rhythm which further intensifies the feeling of anguish.

There are two points to be made about the difference between our pronunciations of words and those common in Shakespeare's time. First, most speakers of English today will say "being" in line 8 as a two-syllable word: "be-ing." But in Shakespeare's time it was probably pronounced as a single-syllable word, so the first scansion treats "being" in that way. But notice – once again – that a scansion of the word as a double rather than single offbeat between "speed" and "made" does not essentially change the rhythm of the line; though the single-offbeat version is more historically correct than the other, both performances are natural sounding, and both are accommodated by beat scansion.

The second point has to do with the word "instinct," meaning an inborn intuitive power. There are two pronunciations of the word in today's usage – **in**stinct and in**stinct** – but they mean different things. In Shakespeare's time, however, the word we pronounce **in**stinct (as in "The child has kind instincts") was pronounced with an emphasis on the second syllable: in**stinct**. So for Shakespeare, line 7 was more evenly regular than a modern reader would hear it. But again, our scansion can accommodate either pronunciation.

Shakespeare wrote in the latter part of the sixteenth century and the beginning of the seventeenth. At the beginning of the eighteenth century, a young poet named Alexander Pope published his *Essay on Criticism*, written using the same five-beat line which, as we've noted, has a long history and is usually called "iambic pentameter" (more on names in Chapter 6). Lines 262 to 265 from Part Two of the *Essay* state notions common in the period when Pope was writing, and they are at the same time good examples of the "art" of metrically regular verse that was popular in his time. The last line, about the sound echoing the sense, is a short, attractive statement of what we have been emphasizing: that meanings and the ways in which they are presented reinforce each other. And as we have noted, sounds and rhythms can even help create meanings.

After writing out these four lines carefully, read them aloud and scan them. Then compare your performance with ours. Where do we differ? Where do you prefer your readings to ours, and how do you explain your preferences?

```
True ease in writing comes from art, not chance,
As those move easiest who have learn'd to dance.
'Tis not enough no harshness gives offence;
The sound must seem an echo to the sense.
```

Here is our performance. The alternate performances that we can hear readily are indicated on additional lines under our preferred scansion. Other natural-sounding performances may be possible.

```
True ease in writing comes from art, not chance,
  O B   o   B o    b      o B    o    B
                                 O

As those move easiest who have learn'd to dance.
o    B   o    B o     b  o    B      o B
         -o-

'Tis not enough no harshness gives offence;
  o   B o B    o B    o    B   o B
          O            b
```

```
The sound must seem an echo to the sense.
  o  B    o   B  o B o  b   o  B
                 b
```

An observation about the alternate scannings of "easiest": here again there are two possible pronunciations of the word, our modern pronunciation with three syllables (eas-ee-est), or another pronunciation with the second and third syllables run together – or elided: eas-yest. Pope, who usually adhered strictly to ten syllables per five-beat line, surely heard, or performed, the two-syllable version. But our scansion accommodates the three-syllable version perfectly well, without at all suggesting a disruption of the basic meter; one simply has a double offbeat in place of a single one, which as we have observed happens frequently. So there is no real problem with the meter. However, the more familiar one becomes with the poetry of earlier periods, the more one will be inclined to respect the strict syllable-counting of poets like Pope by pronouncing such words in the manner that best preserves the meter. (Sometimes, the existence of alternative pronunciations allows a poet to use the same word in two different ways – we'll come across an example by Blake toward the end of this book.)

From our second chapter on, we have made reference to Elizabeth Barrett Browning's poem "How Do I Love Thee? Let Me Count the Ways." Here now is the entire poem – also a sonnet, by the way – for you to copy out, read aloud, and scan.

```
How do I love thee? Let me count the ways.
I love thee to the depth and breadth and height
My soul can reach, when feeling out of sight
For the ends of being and ideal grace.
I love thee to the level of every day's              5
Most quiet need, by sun and candle-light.
I love thee freely, as men strive for right.
I love thee purely, as they turn from praise.
I love thee with the passion put to use
In my old griefs, and with my childhood's faith.    10
I love thee with a love I seemed to lose
With my lost saints. I love thee with the breath,
```

> Smiles, tears, of all my life; and, if God choose,
> I shall but love thee better after death.

This sonnet has a rhyming pattern different from Shakespeare's. Though "rhyme schemes" are not a part of metrical considerations, it's interesting to note that most traditional sonnets (fourteen-lined poems using five-beat lines and rhyme) are written in one of two forms. The form Shakespeare uses is called the English, or, hardly surprisingly, the Shakespearean form. Browning uses the Italian form, often called the Petrarchan form after the great Italian sonneteer who lived between 1304 and 1374, Francesco Petrarca. (We've seen another example in Emma Lazarus's "The New Colossus.") You can easily identify the rhyme schemes, where rhyme words are indicated by letters of the alphabet (**a** rhymes with **a**, **b** with **b**, etc.). Here they are:

Shakespearean: **a b a b c d c d e f e f g g**
Petrarchan: **a b b a a b b a c d c d c d**
or   **c d e c d e**

Notice, incidentally, that in "How Heavy Do I Journey on the Way" the **e**-rhymes are not quite exact: "on" and "groan" don't match exactly in the way the **f**-rhymes "hide" and "side" do. In Shakespeare's day, the sounds were probably closer but still not identical. Is this a problem? Does this slight difference mean that the pattern is broken? No: less-than-perfect matches of sound do not disrupt an overall pattern, or call for additional letters of the alphabet. Perhaps you didn't even notice that slight mismatch in the Shakespeare poem. But you're likely to be more aware of the sound differences in Browning's **a**-rhymes, which are "ways," "grace," "day's," and "praise." The "grace" is a bit further away from "ways" than "groan" is from "on." But, again, there is really no problem. The poet is following the Petrarchan pattern well enough. (The Petrarchan pattern is quite simply harder to use than the Shakespearean pattern since the writer has to find four closely-rhyming words for his or her **a**-rhymes and four more for the **b**-rhymes.)

Here is our performance of the poem, with some alternative possibilities:

```
How do I love thee? Let me count the ways.
 B  -o-  B     o    B  o B     o B
                      b
I love thee to the depth and breadth and height
o B     o  b  o B    o     B    o   B
My soul can reach, when feeling out of sight
 o B    o  B      o   B  o  b  o  B
For the ends of being and ideal grace.
  -o-  B    o  Bo   b   o Bo    B
I love thee to the level of every day's                5
o B     o  b  o B -o-  B o    B
Most quiet need, by sun and candle-light.
 O   B o  B    o  B o    B  o B
I love thee freely, as men strive for right.
o B     o   B  o b   o    B   o  B
              B  -o-   B ô  B
I love thee purely, as they turn from praise.
o B     o   B  o b   o   B    o   B
I love thee with the passion put to use
o B     o  b    o B o   B  o B
In my old griefs, and with my childhood's faith.   10
o  B O    B    o   b   o  B  o     B
 -o-  B  ô  B
I love thee with a love I seemed to lose
o B     o  b  o B o B    o B
With my lost saints. I love thee with the breath,
 o   B O   B      o B   o  b   o  B
   -o-   B ô B
Smiles, tears, of all my life; and, if God choose,
 O     B    o B   o B   o   B   O    B
                        B    -o-   B ô B
I shall but love thee better after death.
o  b   o  B   o  B  o B o   B
B    -o-
```

Although there are two possible pronunciations of "ideal" in line four – "**i**-deal" and "i-**de**-al" – the meter demands the second, or else the line falls into the familiar (but here unwanted) four-beat rhythm:

```
For the ends of being and ideal grace
  -o-    B    o    B  -o-    B o      B
```

This four-beat possibility that can suggest itself when there is any freeing up of the pentameter is usually carefully avoided by poets writing five-beat verse.

The alternative scansions of the last line represent two different ideas about how the poem ends – ideas that arise from somewhat different readings of the poem's meaning. One of us finds the poem ending on a calm note as the poet contemplates a life to come in contrast to the stresses of life on earth, palpable in the jagged rhythms of the two previous lines. The other feels an underlying threat of a death that, rather than uniting, might separate the lovers, and hence prefers an energetic final "I" on the part of a poet determined to assert what she can only hope is true.

The five-beat line has been used in all sorts of rhymed poems and in plays, long narratives, and philosophical poems, these usually being unrhymed. (Four-beat verse is hardly ever unrhymed; it seems that the stronger, simpler rhythm leads us to expect the ends of lines, or pairs of lines, to rhyme.) The unrhymed five-beat, or iambic pentameter, line – called **blank verse** – is the medium for innumerable meditations and narrations, for epics like Milton's *Paradise Lost*, published in 1667, and autobiographies like Wordsworth's *Prelude*. (The label "blank verse" was devised because, while many iambic pentameter poems are rhymed, this particular sort of unrhymed verse has a "blank" where we might expect rhyme.) Lines 248 to 251 from *Paradise Lost*, Book Four, will provide an example of blank verse. You will note that Milton uses highly impressive and dignified language here in his first description of Eden, the paradise of Adam and Eve, which he calls "A happy rural seat of various view":

```
Groves whose rich trees wept odorous gums and balm;
  B        -o=      B   O   B o      B   o   B
                                  -o-

Others whose fruit, burnished with golden rind,
B   -o-      B [o] B      -o-     B  o   B

Hung amiable — Hesperian fables true,
  O   B o  b    o  B o    B  o    B
      -o-

If true, here only — and of delicious taste.
 o    B   O   B o  b   -o- B o      B
              -o-    b  o
```

The richness and complexity of Milton's meter in these lines help to create a sense of the gorgeousness of the garden from which Adam and Eve will eventually be expelled. Would rhyming have made the lines more poetic? Probably not; the blank verse seems suited to this long and varied narrative.

You will note that in our performance of the first line above we've given, as an alternative possibility, a three-syllable pronunciation for the word "odorous," which is the most usual way of pronouncing the word today. But a poet in the period when Milton was writing would have elided the vowel in "-dor-" – that is, run the syllables together to say "o-drous." In the third line, where Milton inserts a remark which distinguishes the true "golden fruit" of Eden from the false "golden apples" of the Garden of the Hesperides in Greek mythology, we have another example of this kind of elision; here "amiable" has three, rather than four, syllables: "a-mya-ble" rather than "a-mi-a-ble." But because of the natural rhythms of spoken English, the regularity of the meter isn't compromised if a more modern pronunciation is used – the result is simply the occurrence of double instead of single offbeats. And Milton would also have elided what we would probably perform as three syllables ("on-ly-and") into two ("on-lyand"). But performing the lines either with or without such elisions is not likely to change our perception of the five beats in these elegant lines.

Even today narrative poems are written using blank verse, and a notable one is by the contemporary poet Mary Jo Salter. As several of our earlier examples have been written by Robert Frost, it seems apt to quote the final section of "Frost at Midnight," a 173-line poem Ms. Salter wrote about him. (The title, punning on *frost*, is identical with that of a blank verse poem by Samuel Taylor Coleridge, the Romantic poet best known for "The Rime of the Ancient Mariner.") In these lines the poet is on his deathbed reading a letter from his daughter Lesley, who calls her father "lion-hearted" (like Richard Coeur de Lion, King of England in the 1190s). The poem's meter varies from a strict offbeat-beat pattern to much looser arrangements, but the form is held to in a manner that honors her poem's subject. Compare the scansion of your performance with ours, which follows below. Incidentally, the remark in the second line about tossing a coin refers to the fact that when he was determined to leave New Hampshire at the age of thirty-eight, Frost had tossed a coin to decide between going for several years to Canada or to England, and England had won.

```
Now Frost is eighty-eight. He can see ahead.
Poet of chance and choice, who tossed a coin
but knew which side his bread was buttered on,
who said, "The most inalienable right of man
is to go to hell in his own way," here he is        5
in a hospital bed, a hell he hasn't made.
He has a letter from Lesley, who knows him for
the stubborn vanities and selfless gestures.
She knows, dear girl, the words to make him well,
if anything can make him well. She calls him        10
"Robert Coeur de Lion." Too weak to write,
he dictates a final letter back to her.
"You're something of a Lesley de Lion
yourself," he says, and he commends the children's
poems she's been working on. It's good              15
to have a way with the young. The old man
hasn't lost his knack, even in prose,
for giving the truth the grandeur of a cadence.
"I'd rather be taken for brave than anything else."
```

Ms. Salter's lines develop a contemporary conversational tone by using many of the possibilities for varying five-beat lines. Here is a possible performance. You will note that the fourth line contains an instance of the very rare triple offbeat; in a stricter style of blank verse it would not occur. There are also many double offbeats, which, although more common than triple offbeats, are, as we have seen, used in the strictest blank verse only in combinations with implied or virtual beats in such a way as to keep the number of syllables in the line constant. Note, too, that the French pronunciation of "Lion" isn't "**li**on", but "lee**on**."

```
Now Frost is eighty-eight. He can see ahead.
 o   B   o   B   o  B      -o-    B  o B
 O   B

Poet of chance and choice, who tossed a coin
 B -o-   B    o    B     o  B    o B

but knew which side his bread was buttered on,
 o   B    o    B    o    B    o   B  o   b

who said, "The most inalienable right of man
  o   B     o  B   o B   ~o~    B   o   B

is to go to hell in his own way," here he is      5
 -o-   B  o B   -o-   B   O    B    o B

in a hospital bed, a hell he hasn't made.
 -o-  B  -o-   B   o  B   o  B o   B

He has a letter from Lesley, who knows him for
 o  B  o B  -o-    B    -o-    B    o   b

the stubborn vanities and selfless gestures.
  o   B  o    B o b  o    B  o    B  o

She knows, dear girl, the words to make him well,
  o   B    O    B     o  B    o  B   o   B

if anything can make him well. She calls him     10
 o  B o  b   o   B   o  B     o  B    o

"Robert Coeur de Lion." Too weak to write,
  B  o   B   -o- B    O   B   o   B

he dictates a final letter back to her.
  o  B    -o- B o  B  o   B    o  B
 -o-    B    o
```

```
"You're something of a Lesley de Lion
 O      B    o   b  o  B  o   b  oB

yourself," he says, and he commends the children's
 o  B      o B    o    B  o B      o  B   o

poems she's been working on. It's good          15
Bo     B    o    B  o   B   O    B

to have a way with the young. The old man
 o  B   a B    -o-      B       o B  ô B

hasn't lost his knack, even in prose,
 B  o   B   o   B [o]B -o-    B

for giving the truth the grandeur of a cadence.
 o   B  -o-    B    o   B  o   b  o  B o

"I'd rather be taken for brave than anything else."
 o    B   -o-  B  -o-    B     o  B -o-    B
```

Notice in line 15 that "poems" is scanned as a two-syllable word, although some people would normally use a one-syllable pronunciation. We could pronounce it this way, as "pomes," and perform the line with an implied offbeat between "poems" and "she's." But it's likely that instead of sensing the necessary pause which an implied offbeat suggests, we would experience a four-beat line:

```
Poems she's been working on. It's good
B         -o-    B  o   b   o    B
```

So the two-syllable pronunciation is the one that easily keeps to the five-beat norm of the poem – and it's likely to be Ms. Salter's pronunciation. (Several months after we had completed these remarks, we spoke with the poet and learned that, yes, she would say "po-ems," thus giving the nine-syllable line its five-beat, rather than four-beat, performance.)

FURTHER PRACTICE

1 An additional Petrarchan sonnet

We noticed that Elizabeth Barrett Browning's "How Do I Love Thee" is a sonnet written in the Petrarchan, or Italian, form (p. 65) – as is Emma Lazarus's "The New Colossus. (Again, see the "Names and labels" chapter for further information about stanza-forms.) Here is a second poem using the form by Gwendolyn Brooks, the first black woman to receive the Pulitzer Prize – for her 1949 book *Annie Allen*, in which this poem, "The Rites for Cousin Vit," appeared. The vitality of Cousin Vit, whose death simply cannot be admitted, is suggested not only by the vivid details of her life and imagined afterlife, but by the clearly metered yet almost breathless half-sentences – particularly the final one. Scan the poem to determine how words variously emphasized within the careful structure add energy and interest to what we learn of Cousin Vit, and of the poet's attitude toward her life. Note how the word "haply," which simply means "perhaps," seems particularly cheerful when used in close connection with "happiness."

```
Carried her unprotesting out the door.
Kicked back the casket-stand. But it can't hold her,
That stuff and satin aiming to enfold her,
The lid's contrition nor the bolts before.
Oh oh. Too much. Too much. Even now, surmise,     5
She rises in the sunshine. There she goes,
Back to the bars she knew and the repose
In love-rooms and the things in people's eyes.
Too vital and too squeaking. Must emerge.
Even now she does the snake-hips with a hiss,    10
Slops the bad wine across her shantung, talks
Of pregnancy, guitars and bridgework, walks
In parks or alleys, comes haply on the verge
Of happiness, haply hysterics. Is.
```

Here is our scansion of the poem, with alternative performances for several lines:

Carried her unprotesting out the door.
 B   -o-   b   o B o   B   o B

Kicked back the casket-stand. But it can't hold her,
 B   =o-   B o   B   o B o   B   o
 O   B   o   -o-   B ô B

That stuff and satin aiming to enfold her,
  O   B o   B o B o   b o B   o

The lid's contrition nor the bolts before.
  o B   o   B o b   o B   o B

Oh oh. Too much. Too much. Even now, surmise,   5
 O B   O B   O B   =o-   B   o B

She rises in the sunshine. There she goes,
  o B o b   o B o   B   o B

Back to the bars she knew and the repose
 B   -o-   B   o   B o   b o B

In love-rooms and the things in people's eyes.
 o   B ô B   -o-   B   o B o B
    B   o   b   o B

Too vital and too squeaking. Must emerge.
 O   B o b   o   B   o   B   o B
    -o-   B ô B

Even now she does the snake-hips with a hiss,   10
=o-   B   o B   o B ô B   -o-   B
                o   B   o   b o B

Slops the bad wine across her shantung, talks
  B   -o=   B o B   o   B o   B

Of pregnancy, guitars and bridgework, walks
 o   B o b o B o   B   O   B
                              o

In parks or alleys, comes haply on the verge
 o B   o B   -o-   B o b   o B
         B   -o=   B

Of happiness, haply hysterics. Is.
 o B   o B [o] B -o-   B o   B

You may have discovered that the last line – culminating with that astonishing single-word single-beat sentence, "Is" – is easily experienced as the more song-like four-beat line unless we give greater emphasis than usual to "ness" in "happiness." Here's how that four-beat performance would be scanned:

```
Of happiness, haply hysterics. Is.
o   B -o-    B  -o-  B o    B
```

It's doubtful, though, that Gwendolyn Brooks – conscious of the long tradition of sonnet writing to which she is contributing – would depart from the meter of the previous thirteen lines when her ear could hear, and her pulses feel, a five-beat performance of the line. As we said much earlier on, poets writing in regular meters tend to stick to the patterns they've established. In any case, an energetic sonnet like this one of Brooks's will have a variety of performances, but a calm and entirely regular one will not be among them.

2 A writing exercise

Perhaps you would like to try writing a traditional sonnet yourself. You know what the game plan is: iambic pentameter, fourteen lines, either the Shakespearean pattern or the Petrarchan. You can begin with a line you like and carry on, seeing where your inspiration takes you. Or, you can play a different sort of game. With a friend or friends, or in a class, choose a group of words at random and then commit yourself to using them as rhyme words in the poem you will write. This may sound bizarre, but many have discovered that by having to write toward a specific word, and then find a word to rhyme with it a line or two later, one can come up with more interesting material than if one is "freer." The results can be surprisingly varied, and surprisingly successful. Here is an example, written in the Shakespearean style by a student, Michelle Guerard, to these chosen-at-random words, each of which required finding a matching rhyme word: smoking/right, lake/see, style/pair, weeping. Guerard's poem is called "Neighbors."

I see my neighbor at the window smoking,
A pack of filtered Salems to her right.
I know she hears our laughing and our joking.
She sits across the alley every night.

And now she hears us chat about the lake.   5
I speak of sights in ways that let her see.
I crack the window more, as cookies bake.
The smell will drift. I pour a cup of tea.

Winds lift her curtains, sadly out of style.
A gold band glitters, once part of a pair.   10
But someone said he's been gone quite a while;
I wonder how they lived, what did they share?

In bed I lie, with sounds of someone weeping.
Thoughts turn to me, and what it is I'm seeking.

Particularly effective for us are the rhythmic patterns in lines 9 through 12. In line 9 we feel an initial emphasis on "winds" in "Winds lift her curtains." That emphasis, followed by a double offbeat whose first part, "lift," is also emphasized in our performance, gives a strong and energetic opening to the line and, for us, helps to create a sense of sudden freshness. Line 10's "gold band glitters" – three emphasized words – suggests the importance of the wedding ring and what it once represented; then the implied offbeat between "once" and "part" helps to convey separation, a feeling enhanced by the double offbeat that separates "part" and "pair." Then, in line 12, the virtual offbeat at the comma conveys a sense of the imagination's hesitation between two thoughts. Here's our scansion of these lines:

```
Winds lift her curtains, sadly out of style.
 B       =o-    B  o      B  o b   o    B
A gold band glitters, once part of a pair.          10
o B   0    B o    B   ô B    -o-   B
But someone said he's been gone quite a while;
 o  B  o    B    o    B    0     B  o   B
I wonder how they lived, what did they share?
o  B  o    B    o    B  [o] B    -o-     B
```

RHYTHMIC FIGURES 5

Poets writing in regular meters can vary their patterning of empha-
sized and unemphasized syllables only within strict limits, or else
the lines will cease to be metrical or will be heard as some other
meter (as when five-beat lines collapse into a four-beat rhythm). In
exploiting these limited possibilities, poets down the centuries have
used the same short metrical sequences time and time again, and
in scanning and responding to metrical poetry it's helpful to be able
to recognize them and understand some of their uses. We call these
mini-patterns **rhythmic figures**, and in this chapter we'll ask you to
look at, and listen to, the most common of them. The five major
figures have already been encountered in earlier chapters, though
we didn't dwell on them there; now we can revisit some of those
examples with a different purpose. Two of these figures involve three
syllables – **o b o** and **B O B** – and the other three involve four syllables
– **B** -o- **B**, -o- **B ô B**, and **B ô B** -o-.

1 o b o

Again and again, it has become clear that syllables without any partic-
ular emphasis can be felt as beats. Here are some examples:

Frost, "Stopping by Woods on a Snowy Evening":

```
The darkest evening of the year.
              o   b   o
```

Lazarus, "The New Colossus":

```
A mighty woman with a torch, whose flame
          o   b   o
```

Wordsworth, "I Wandered Lonely as a Cloud":

```
Fluttering and dancing in the breeze
          o    b     o
```

In these examples, the words we've marked as **b** are all words normally pronounced very lightly. In reading these lines, there's no need to give them extra emphasis: because of the situation in which we encounter them, they can happily function as beats in the rhythm of the line as long as they are not rushed in pronunciation. That situation is evident from these examples – between two other lightly pronounced syllables that are functioning as offbeats.

There is one other place where a beat on a syllable which is not emphasized is easily felt, and that's at the end of the line:

```
A host, of golden daffodils;
        o b
```

Again, a performance doesn't have to give an artificial emphasis to the last syllable of "daffodils"; because it falls between an unemphasized syllable functioning as an offbeat and the end of the line, the beat is felt when the word is given a normal pronunciation.

It is often tempting to give a little extra weight to these **b**'s to help bring out the alternating pattern of the meter, and in some instances this can be justified. The more appropriate a chant-like reading is, the more one can add a bit of emphasis that wouldn't be there in a prose version. In *The Song of Hiawatha*, a poem which imitates the meter of a Finnish epic, the American poet Henry Wadsworth Longfellow (1807–82) uses lines whose norm is to begin with beats, even when they're unemphatic words:

```
Listen to this Indian Legend,
 B  o   b   o  B  o   B o
To this Song of Hiawatha!
 b   o  B   o  Bo B  o
```

Neither "to" in these lines would be stressed in prose, which is why we mark them **b** rather than **B**. But one kind of performance of the poem would give them at least a certain degree of emphasis.

You may notice, by the way, that just as the last syllable of a line of verse whose norm is to begin with an offbeat can be an unemphasized **b**, the first syllable of a line whose norm is to begin with a beat can also be an unemphasized **b**. (The usual labeling of these two kinds of verse as "iambic" and "**trochaic**" will be discussed in our next chapter.)

When, however, the poet is not seeking a chant-like performance but is imitating closely the sounds and rhythmic movements of spoken English, it's much more appropriate to leave **b**'s as unemphasized. Here's Shakespeare's Hamlet:

```
Whether 'tis nobler in the mind to suffer
                  o  b    o
The slings and arrows of outrageous fortune
                  o   b o
```

It would be painful to have to listen to an actor who thought it was right to emphasize "in" and "of" in these lines!

The rhythmic effect of using many **b**'s is often to speed the words up and lighten the movement of the verse, as they provide a way of keeping the rhythm going without the weight of many emphasized syllables. If you look back at Wordsworth's "I Wandered Lonely as a Cloud," you'll see that the sprightly lilt of that poem comes partly from the considerable number of **b**'s, either in the **o b o** sequence or in **o b** at the end of the line.

2 **B O B**

Our next rhythmic figure is the mirror-image of the previous one. Just as an unemphasized syllable can function as a beat when it comes between similarly unemphasized syllables (or at the end of a line), so an emphasized syllable can function as an *offbeat* if it has emphasized beats on both sides. We've already encountered many examples, including these:

Herrick, "To the Virgins, to Make Much of Time":

```
And this same flower that smiles today
       B   O     B
```

Hardy, "I Look into My Glass":

```
For then, I, undistressed
      B   O B
By hearts grown cold to me,
      B     O     B
```

Dickinson, "I Like a Look of Agony":

```
The Eyes glaze once — and that is Death —
      B     O  B
```

Once again, there's no need to give an artificial pronunciation to bring out the alternating pattern of beat-offbeat-beat: the natural rhythm of spoken English, working with the expectations the poem has already set up, will do the job for us. Many of these words *demand* a strong emphasis. If we don't stress "same" in Herrick's line, we lose the emphatic point the poet is making about the short-lived beauty of the flower; if we don't give "glaze" as much weight as "Eyes" and "once" in Dickinson's line, we short-change a powerful description of dying. The commas around Hardy's "I" show that it must be emphasized. Only "grown" could perhaps be spoken with less of a thump than its neighbors, if we wanted to put more emphasis on "cold" – though we'd still probably want to scan it as **O**, since it keeps much of its normal weight.

Emphasized offbeats are also possible at the beginning of the line, before an emphasized beat. (You can see how similar this is to the occurrence of **b** at the end of a line after an **o**):

Lazarus, "The New Colossus":

```
Send these, the homeless, tempest-tost to me,
 O    B
```

Hardy, "I Look into My Glass":

```
Part steals, lets part abide;
 O     B
```

Because the **B O B** figure produces three heavy syllables in a row (or two in the case of **O B** at the start of the line), it often has the effect of slowing down the movement of the words. We've already pointed out how appropriate this can be in the made-up example we used to introduce the emphasized offbeat: "But when the **clock winds down**." Hearts growing cold and eyes glazing are also events that happen slowly, and are evoked slowly in the lines by Hardy and Dickinson.

3 B -o- B

Another very common rhythmic figure in verse where the lines normally start with an offbeat is the **B -o- B** figure. When this figure occurs, as it very often does, at the beginning of the line, it is called "initial inversion" because it inverts, or reverses, the expected sequence of offbeat–beat. We've already observed how frequently initial inversion occurs; here are some of our many examples:

Herrick, "To Virgins, to Make Much of Time":

```
Gather ye rosebuds while ye may
 B   -o-   B
```

Lazarus, "The New Colossus":

```
Here at our sea-washed, sunset gates shall stand
 B     -o-    B
```

Wordsworth, "I Wandered Lonely as a Cloud":

```
Fluttering and dancing in the breeze
 B       -o-    B
```

("Fluttering," here, is pronounced as two syllables; if pronounced as three syllables, the triple-offbeat sign would be used: ~**o**~.)

Dickinson, "I Like a Look of Agony":

```
Men do not sham Convulsion
 B   -o-     B
```

The **B** -o- **B** initial inversion is so familiar that it doesn't necessarily have a direct impact on the meaning of the line in which it occurs. But if the opening word is one that gains from a little extra rhythmic prominence – like "gather" and "fluttering" in our first and third examples – then this way of starting a line notably enhances that word's expressive power.

Another rhythmic figure, which feels just like the **B** -o- **B** initial inversion, happens *within* lines of regular meter. It's as though an initial inversion is occurring *not* at the beginning of the line, but after a break caused by a virtual beat – as though the line were beginning again. If one needed to give it a name, the figure might be called medial (or "in the middle") inversion. We've seen it many times, first encountering it in our chapter on basic rhythms: "The **ways** she **count**-ed **beats**, **so** that her **praise**." This figure occurs when we have, *first*, a virtual offbeat after a beat (often signaled by a punctuation mark), and *second*, the **B** -o- **B** figure.

Describing how this figure works and feels is more involved than hearing it. Perform the following examples aloud, with energy; the figure's rhythmical pattern will be clear. These famous lines are spoken by Shakespeare's Macbeth in a moment of horror and defiance:

```
Is this a dagger, which I see before me?
The handle toward my hand? Come, let me clutch thee!
                 B  [o]B        -o-     B
```

Wordsworth's *Prelude* gives us another instance:

```
Shouldering the naked crag, oh, at that time
                    B[o]B     -o-     B
```

And we discussed another line of his that uses it:

```
My horse moved on; hoof after hoof
          B [o]B      -o-    B
```

Milton, in *Paradise Lost*, extracts a different quality from the same figure:

```
Others whose fruit, burnished with golden rind,
         B [o] B        -o-      B
```

It's easy to feel the same rhythm at play here as in our examples from the beginnings of lines. An essential difference, though, is that in these cases the **B** -o- **B** figure is preceded by a real break in the rhythm, and this can be used for dramatic effect – as in the first two of our examples. The speaker in each of these lines stops for a moment, and then plunges on with an exclamation: "Come, let me clutch thee!"; "oh, at that time." You won't expect this rhythmic figure to occur very often in poetry that imitates song, but when an energetic speaking voice is being heard in the verse, its use is particularly effective.

Occasionally the double offbeat associated with the **B** -o- **B** figure has a little more weight on one or other of its syllables. In the Wordsworth line you might, for instance, want to give "that" in "oh, at that time" a bit of emphasis. You know already how to show this in the scansion: **B** -o= **B**.

4 -o- B ô B

Our next rhythmic figure embraces four syllables, and moves smoothly from a double offbeat to a pair of emphasized beats separated only by an implied offbeat – the slight pause induced by the side-by-side beats.

Lazarus, "The New Colossus":

```
The air-bridged harbor that twin cities frame.
                    -o-        B ô B
```

Wordsworth, "Strange Fits of Passion":

```
All over the wide lea
    -o-     B  ô B
```

Shakespeare, Sonnet 29:

```
When, in disgrace with Fortune and men's eyes
                            -o-     B    ôB
```

This rhythmic figure mounts a challenge to the smoothness of the meter: first the double offbeat postpones the expected beat, then the two emphasized beats momentarily retard the onward movement. The implied offbeat that separates them doesn't do more than the minimum necessary to keep a sense of alternation going. It's a figure poets will use sparingly – too many of these, and the meter will break down. But used carefully, it can add greatly to the verse's evocation of emotion, imitation of movement, and emulation of the speaking voice. How it does this will, of course, be a product of the specific words the poet chooses.

5 B ô B -o-

Our final rhythmic figure is the reverse of the previous one. Now the pair of beats, with the implied offbeat separating them, is followed by the double offbeat. This is the least common of our five figures, but Shakespeare's Sonnet 50 uses it a surprising four times, at least if we opt for it and for the modern pronunciation of "instinct" over other possible readings:

```
As if by some instinct the wretch did know
          B   ôB       -o-

The bloody spur cannot provoke him on
          B ô B    -o-

That sometimes anger thrusts into his hide;
             B    ôB  -o-

For that same groan doth put this in my mind-
             B ô  B    -o-
```

The challenge to a smooth alternating rhythm is even stronger with this figure than with the previous one, as there's no double offbeat to ease the way into the disruptive pair of emphasized beats. Only *after* the beat, implied offbeat, beat sequence does a double offbeat come to lighten and restore the regular meter. This degree of rhythmic tension is entirely appropriate for a poem expressing pain and grief.

This figure is related to our third rhythmic figure, **B -o- B**, when it occurs within the line – it is, that is to say, a type of medial inversion.

In the earlier case, the figure is preceded by a break [o]. In this final figure it is preceded only by an implied offbeat – the slowing down of the rhythm produced by two side-by-side beats – and not a break, and the result is a quite different rhythmic feeling. Instead of experiencing a rhythmic unit that starts between the beats, we experience one that starts with the two side-by-side beats.

You will discover that occasionally there are lines which do not definitely fall into one pattern or the other – where the unpronounced offbeat might either be implied or virtual, depending on whether or not your performance has a break. But the differences in the way the rhythm operates, and therefore the meanings it conveys, are usually very marked. Compare the last line quoted above with this rewritten version:

```
For that same groan doth show: this is my mind-
                    B [o] B    -o-
```

Here both "show" and "this" have their own rhythmic space, with a virtual offbeat taking up the pause in between. In both versions the alternating rhythm is put under some strain, but the first seems more uncertain and tense, the second more assertive and clear-cut – and less appropriate for the mood of the sonnet.

With these five rhythmic figures we have identified the vast majority of variations from regular meter – the straightforward alternation of o and B – in English verse, and most of the other, less common figures involve variations upon these variations that move them a bit further away from regularity (for instance, by using =o- and -o=, or by separating the double offbeat and its accompanying virtual or implied offbeat by a few syllables).

There is no code that will assign specific meanings to each of these rhythmic figures. Although it's possible to generalize, as we have done, about the meanings and the feelings they may suggest – like tension, or sprightliness, or speed – the figures are always used in particular contexts, and embodied in particular words, to produce unique effects that can't be legislated for in advance, and which individual performances may define differently.

As a demonstration of how a poet may use these common rhythmic patterns in a poem, here is one stanza of the "Ode on Melancholy" by the English Romantic poet John Keats (1795–1821). In this stanza the speaker urges anyone who is subject to an unexplained fit of melancholy to increase that "anguished" but "wakeful" mood by contemplating the purest forms of beauty. The meter is the familiar five-beat iambic pentameter line, and we have scanned only the syllables that occur in rhythmic figures, with underlining to show the figures more clearly.

```
But when the melancholy fit shall fall
o    b    o      o    b o

    Sudden from heaven like a weeping cloud,
    B    -o-    B  o   b  o

That fosters the droop-headed flowers all,
          -o-    B  ô B

    And hides the green hill in an April shroud;
                B ô B    -o-

Then glut thy sorrow on a morning rose,
              o  b o

    Or on the rainbow of the salt sand-wave,
    o  b    o      o  b   o B   O   B

        Or on the wealth of globèd peonies;
        o  b   o                  o b

Or if thy mistress some rich anger shows,
o  b    o          B   O   B

    Emprison her soft hand, and let her rave,
        -o-    B ô B

    And feed deep, deep upon her peerless eyes.
        B   O   B   o  b   o
```

Every line uses one or more of the rhythmic figures we have been looking at, and all five figures are used in the stanza (though **B -o- B** occurs only as initial inversion, not as a medial inversion). One effect is to vary the pace of the poem: it moves quickly over less important material by using frequent **o b o** figures, and dwells on significant phrases by bringing **B**'s together, either in -o- **B ô B** or **B ô B** -o- pairs ("droop-headed," "green hill," "soft hand"), or through the use of the emphasized offbeat in the **B O B** figure ("salt sand-wave," "some rich anger," "feed deep, deep"). This variation in pace contributes to the richness of the poem's texture, a richness which provides us with one more example of intense beauty to add to those it mentions. And the concrete images are all the more vividly realized when the rhythmic figures encourage the performer to linger over the words that present them.

NAMES AND LABELS 6

Throughout our discussion of poetic meter and the beat–offbeat method of scansion, we have principally used labels like "four-beat line" or "five-beat line." The reason for this is probably clear. Since the rule for meter in English is that **rhythm in English poetry is realized by the alternation of beats and offbeats**, we wished to use labels that would continually reinforce this basic understanding. You have probably noticed, though, that from time to time the label "iambic pentameter" has slipped in during discussions of the kinds of five-beat lines to which we have paid considerable attention, as in Shakespeare's and Browning's sonnets.

In our Introduction we described our dissatisfaction with Greek labels like iamb, trochee, and anapest, and how we found scansion by beats and offbeats much more helpful in reading and enjoying actual poems. Yet having learned to understand and work with these simpler, more useful concepts, we can admit another truth: those Greek words have been in use for a long time in discussions of poetry, and as labels – rather than as keys to what's really going on in metrical lines – they can be a useful shorthand for describing particular sorts of meters.

So in this chapter we will discuss some common names and labels. But nothing more complex will have to be learned about scansion; that job has been done. And if any of these names and labels seem to complicate your life unnecessarily, don't worry. If you've improved your hearing of the rhythms of metrical poems in English, and if you've learned how, with beat scansion, to share in written form the essentials of your performances, you've eaten the cake – all the rest is icing.

Here are some of the most useful names and labels for talking about poems. We'll look at them in categories: line-length labels, predominant-meter labels, and form and stanza labels.

LINE-LENGTH LABELS

monometer   This "meter" would have a single beat in each line, and as you might imagine, not much can be done with it. It's mentioned only for the sake of completeness. Here's a quick monometer poem, with beats on the second syllable of each line:

```
This verse
will not
reveal
a lot.
```

dimeter   The two-beat line has more possibilities. We encountered it in our First Poem with "We'll talk about beat." Two-beat lines often combine to produce four-beat units, as in limericks.

trimeter   The three-beat line is the norm for our "Hickory dickory dock" poem, and for the shorter lines of Herrick's, Dickinson's, Wordsworth's, and Hardy's poems: for example, "Old time is still a-flying," "We talked between the Rooms," "He raised, and never stopped," "I look into the glass," "Men do not sham Convulsion." (However, virtual beats, **[B]**, are often sensed at the ends of lines where only three beats are represented by spoken syllables, as is particularly evident in ballad stanzas.)

tetrameter   The four-beat line. "Tetra" in Greek means "four," and we use it today in many compound words like "tetragon," a four-sided polygon (a square, for example). "Whose words these are perhaps you know" was the first of our many tetrameter lines.

pentameter   The five-beat line. We encounter "penta" in such words as "pentagon." When "Elizabeth Barrett Browning counted ways" that she loved her husband, she used by far the most common pentameter line – iambic pentameter – for her sonnet.

hexameter   As you can probably guess, this is the six-beat line. Its use in English poetry is relatively rare. Most often one finds it at the conclusion of pentameter stanzas where a strong sense of completing one stanza before moving on to the next is needed, or where the longer line serves as a refrain, as in these two concluding lines from the first stanza of a poem written in the 1590s, the English poet Edmund Spenser's marriage song "Epithalamion":

```
So I unto myself alone will sing;
 o B o   b   o B   o B   o    B
The woods shall to me answer, and my echo ring.
  o  B     o    b  o B   o   b    o B  o B
```

We could go on to "heptameter" (seven-beat) and "octameter" (eight-beat) lines, but poems written in such lines are not often encountered. You will recognize them if you do meet up with them – they're *long*. And they tend to be felt metrically as two shorter lines (trimeters and tetrameters) run together.

PREDOMINANT-METER LABELS

There are many types of verse other than those that we have been discussing, like quantitative, **syllabic**, and strong-stress verse – and, of course, that type so familiar in what many think of as "our" literary period: **free verse**, which has no regular meter based on beats and offbeats. But here are the labels applied to those sorts of meters that are a principal concern of this book. The first four, "iambic," "trochaic," "**anapestic**," and "**dactylic**," are often referred to as **syllable-stress** or **accentual-syllabic** meters, particularly by those who use the foot-scansion derived from Greek and Roman versification. Iambic and trochaic meters are **duple**, because they are based on a movement between single beats and single offbeats; anapestic and dactylic meters are **triple**, because they are based on a movement between single beats and double offbeats.

iambic This word is used along with a line-length label to indicate the norm, or standard pattern, of a poem whose meter rises from offbeat to beat (da-**da**, da-**da**). It is therefore sometimes called a "rising" meter. More poems by well-known poets are written in iambic meters than in any other kind.

A standard *iambic trimeter* line will begin with an offbeat; it will then have three pronounced beats with offbeats between them.

```
But Time, to make me grieve
 o  B    o B   o  B
```

A standard *iambic tetrameter* line will begin with an offbeat and have four beats with offbeats between them.

```
I wandered lonely as a cloud
o B o    B   o b o   B

I died for Beauty — but was scarce
o B   o B   o   b   o    B
```

A standard *iambic pentameter* line will begin with an offbeat and have five beats with offbeats between them.

```
My grief lies onward and my joy behind.
 o  B   o  B  o   b   o B  o B

She knows, dear girl, the words to make him well,
  o   B   O   B    o B    o B   o  B
```

Note, however, that iambic lines may end with an additional offbeat (usually single, but occasionally double):

```
The slings and arrows of outrageous fortune
 o  B    o  B  o   b o  B  o   B  o
```

(The noun *iamb* is used in traditional foot-scansion. An iamb is an individual unit of a line of verse which has an unstressed syllable followed by a stressed one.)

trochaic   This word is used along with a line-length label to indicate the norm, or standard pattern, of a poem whose meter falls from beat to offbeat (**da**-da, **da**-da). It is therefore sometimes called a "falling" meter. A number of poems by well-known poets are written in trochaic meters, though the strictest sorts of trochaic verse, where every line ends with its "**da**-da," are rare. (It is not unusual for the final offbeat of a trochaic line to be omitted, opening the possibility of calling a poem where such lines occur frequently an iambic one with its first offbeats missing; or, more simply, four-beat verse beginning and ending on the beat.) A notable *trochaic trimeter* poem – with *iambic hexameter* lines at the ends of the stanzas – is to "To a Skylark" by the English Romantic poet Percy Bysshe Shelley (1792–1822), which concludes in this way:

```
Teach me half the gladness
 B    o B    o  B o
   That thy brain must know,
      b   o B   o     B
Such harmonious madness
 B    o B o    B o
   From my lips would flow
      b  o B   o     B
The world would listen then – as I am listening now.
   o B     o     B o   B    o B o  B    o    B
```

Most trochaic poems are written in tetrameters. A standard *trochaic tetrameter* line will begin with a beat and have four beats with offbeats between them. In these examples from the "Introduction" to Longfellow's *Hiawatha* (79–87) every line completes this pattern with a final offbeat:

```
Ye who love a nation's legends,
 B  o B  o B  o    B o
Love the ballads of a people, . . .
 B    o B o  b  o B  o
Listen to this Indian Legend,
 B  o b  o B o    B o
To this Song of Hiawatha!
 b  o   B  o  Bo B  o
```

It's very tempting to read "To" in the last line as if it were a strongly stressed word: this is because Longfellow has chosen a line that usually has a more thumping rhythm than iambic lines.

(The noun *trochee* is used in traditional foot-scansion. A trochee is an individual unit of a line of verse which has a stressed syllable followed by an unstressed one.)

anapestic This word, like the next one in our list, indicates that a poem is written in a triple meter; that is to say, it has many more double offbeats than single offbeats, producing a distinctive, often jaunty, swing. *Anapestic* (or *anapaestic*) is used along with a line-length label to indicate the norm, or standard pattern, of a *triple-meter* poem with a pattern that rises from two off-beats to a beat (da-da-**da**, da-da-**da**). Like an iambic meter it is therefore called a "rising" meter; and like poems in trochaic meters, poems written in anapestic meters are usually tetrameter poems.

A standard *anapestic tetrameter* line will begin with two offbeats followed by a beat, and have a total of four beats with double offbeats between them. (A common variation is the omission of the first offbeat.) Here are two familiar examples, the first from "A Visit from St. Nicholas," the second from "The Destruction of Sennacherib," by another English Romantic poet, George Gordon, Lord Byron (1788–1824):

```
'Twas the night before Christmas, when all through the house
   -o-   B    -o-     B      -o-  B         -o-   B

Not a creature was stirring — not even a mouse;
  -o-   B   -o-    B     -o-    B -o-  B

The stockings were hung by the chimney with care . . .
  o   B    -o-    B    -o-    B   -o-     B


The Assyrian came down like the wolf on the fold,
  -o-  B   -o-     B      -o-   B    -o-   B

And his cohorts were gleaming in purple and gold;
  -o-    B    -o-      B      -o-  B   -o-    B
```

(The noun *anapest* is used in traditional foot-scansion. An anapest is an individual unit of a line of verse which has two unstressed syllables followed by a stressed one.)

dactylic This word is used along with a line-length label to indicate the norm, or standard pattern, of a triple-meter poem whose meter falls from a beat to two offbeats (**da**-da-da, **da**-da-da). Like a trochaic meter it is therefore sometimes called a "falling" meter. The meter is a rare one, used occasionally in tetrameter poems and, in a famous instance, for Longfellow's long narrative poem *Evangeline*. This poem uses *dactylic hexameter*, where a line will begin with a beat followed by two offbeats, and will have a total of six beats, normally with double offbeats between them. (A common variation is the omission of the one of the offbeats.) Here is the first line, followed by two later lines, of *Evangeline*:

```
This is the forest primeval. The murmuring pines and the
  B   -o-   B   -o-   B   -o-   B  -o-    B        -o-
                                                hemlocks. . .
                                                B   o

Loud from its rocky caverns, the deep-voiced neighboring ocean
  B    -o-   B o B   -o-   B   O     B   -o-  B o
Speaks, and in accents disconsolate answers the wail
  B       -o- B    -o-   B -o-   B    -o-    B
                                          of the forest.
                                          -o-   B o
```

(The noun *dactyl* is used in traditional foot-scansion. A dactyl is an individual unit of a line of verse which has a stressed syllable followed by two unstressed ones.)

Two additional Greek names, "**pyrrhic**" (the noun is also "pyrrhic") and "**spondaic**" (the noun is "spondee"), are used in traditional foot scansion but not in beat scansion. A pyrrhic is an individual unit of a line of verse which consists solely of two unstressed syllables. A spondee is an individual unit of a line of verse which consists solely of two stressed syllables.

We have seen innumerable instances where we have *double offbeats* (-**o**-) in the context of a complete poetic line; and we have examined innumerable instances where side-by-side *beats* of one sort or another occur with naturally felt pauses between them (implied offbeats, **B ô B**, or, with a rhythmic break, virtual offbeats, **B [o] B**). Because these are normal occurrences in lines of English metrical verse, "pyrrhic" and "spondaic" as special labels for metrical events are not needed.

STRESS VERSE

We can say about those many poems whose lines all have five beats and which use the offbeat-beat pattern as the poem's norm, "This poem is written in iambic pentameter." We can confidently label poems with the line-length and rhythm of "'Twas the Night Before Christmas" as anapestic tetrameter. And when we encounter a poem that uses a complex stanza pattern with varying line lengths, yet whose lines are all, for example, iambic, we can say, "This poem is written in iambic lines of various lengths," thus pointing out the basis for its metricality and suggesting that it differs from simpler forms.

But there are some poems with very definite rhythms or varying meters which none of the common labels or descriptions seems to fit, and for these the term **stress verse** is used. Here is an example, with our performance. It's the first stanza of "Break, Break, Break" by the English poet (and poet laureate), Alfred, Lord Tennyson (1809–92):

```
Break, break, break,
  B  [o]  B  [o]  B
   On thy cold gray stones, O Sea!
    -o-    B    O    B     o  B
 And I would that my tongue could utter
  -o-  B        -o-   B      o    B  o
   The thoughts that arise in me.
     o    B          -o-  B   o   B
```

The first line is strongly metrical – we easily feel the three pronounced beats. But the line is not iambic; it's not anything for which there is a traditional name. Then the second line begins as though we were to have an anapestic meter; but that stops, and we seem to be in iambic territory. And the situation repeats itself in the subsequent lines. To say the poem is written in, say, anapestic trimeter with a bucketful of variations is to make a poem that is simply and clearly metrical (with three beats to a line) into a terminological guessing game. The label "stress verse" is an appropriate one for this poem.

As a second example of stress verse we have the first and last stanzas of Thomas Hardy's four-stanza poem "During Wind and Rain" (1917), where the poet meditates on childhood events recorded in his deceased wife's diary. Here is a performance of these stanzas from this easy-to-hear-metrically but sometimes hard-to-scan poem. In several instances the poet's meters in the first stanza help to identify patterns in the final stanza; but at some points the scansion is as difficult and troubled as is the poet's melancholy sense that the life he describes may have no residual meaning at all:

```
      They sing their dearest songs —
         o    B    o    B   o    B
      He, she, all of them — yea,
       B[o] B[o]B   -o-       B
      Treble and tenor and bass,
        B  -o-    B  -o-    B
        And one to play;
         o    B   o   B
      With the candles mooning each face. . . .          5
        -o-     B   o   B    -o-     B
        Ah, no; the years O!
        B [o]B   o   B [o]B
 How the sick leaves reel down in throngs!
   B    -o=    B     O    B   o    B
. . .

      They change to a high new house,
         o    B     -o- B   O    B
      He, she, all of them — aye,
       B[o] B[o]B   -o-       B
      Clocks and carpets and chairs
        B   o    B    -o-      B
        On the lawn all day,                              25
        -o-    B   O    B
```

```
And the brightest things that are theirs. . . .
   -o-      B    o     B      -o-      B
   Ah, no; the years, the years;
   B [o]B    o  B       o  B
Down their carved names the rain-drop ploughs.
 B        -o=        B      o  B     o    B
```

The rhythm begins easily enough in each stanza (if we're not worrying about whether it is "iambic" or "trochaic"), with lines of three, four, three, and two beats. That fourth line is something of a surprise, since we would expect a three- or four-beat line at this point. We then seem to launch into another simple pattern beginning with a three-beat line and a couple of double offbeats to provide a bit of a lilt ("With the candles mooning each face"). But the following line brings us to a halt by means of two successive emphasized beats ("Ah, no"), where a comma helps to make this a two-beat rather than a one-beat phrase. With this halt we have a painful reminder that these pleasant scenes are irrecoverably past. Although this four-beat line is metrically similar to the second line of the stanza, it can't be read with the same swing; and whereas the second and fourth, and the third and fifth, lines rhyme in every stanza, within no stanza is there a rhyme for the sixth line. For the desolate sixth lines there are only repetitive echoes, never a consoling rhyme: "ah," "no," "years," "O," "years," "years." And the final line in each stanza rhymes only with the first, further disrupting the pattern of alternating pairs of rhyme-lines. In this poem, the grieving thoughts return only upon themselves.

FORM AND STANZA LABELS

The kinds of labels we've noted so far – line-length labels and predominant-meter labels – are useful to help us put names on the metrical lines we scan and on those poems whose meters are consistent, or on those poems that follow established, conventional patterns. Form and stanza labels, however, sometimes name poems or parts of poems that use a specific meter, and sometimes they don't. For example, the traditional *sonnet* is by definition a fourteen-line poem written in iambic pentameter with either an English or an Italian rhyme scheme. A **quatrain**, on the other hand, will be four lines long, but it might be written in any meter; and the label says nothing about whether or not it is rhymed. (Even though quatrains have usually been metered and rhymed, many contemporary poets write quatrains in free verse.) So although form and stanza labels are not essential in a discussion of meter and scansion, a short list of the most common ones, with definitions and examples, may be useful. Fuller lists and longer explanations are available in many literature textbooks, and in guides, handbooks, and dictionaries of poetic terms.

ballad stanza   A four-line stanza whose first and third lines have four beats (tetrameter) and are usually unrhymed; the second and fourth lines have three pronounced beats (trimeter) and are rhymed. This example is from an anonymous English ballad from the fifteenth century, "The Bailiff's Daughter of Islington":

```
There was a youth, and a well beloved youth,
   o    B  o  B        -o-  B    -o=      B
   And he was an esquire's son,
   o   B   -o-  B  o        B   [B]
He loved the bailiff's daughter dear,
   o  B     o  B  o      B      o  B
   That lived in Islington.
      o    B   o  B  o   b   [B]
```

Notice how the jaunty rhythm of the ballad (which would originally have been sung) encourages the performer to emphasize words that in other contexts would be unemphatic: "was" in the first line and "he" in the second line. There's even a temptation to thump the last syllable of "Islington"!

Stanzas written with the same tetrameter-trimeter alternation but with a very regular iambic offbeat-beat pattern, and where the first and third lines – as well as the second and fourth – rhyme, are often called "common measure" or "common meter." This is because the pattern is used commonly for the stanzas of hymns, which are stricter than the looser ballads. Many consider the distinction to be of little use, and call both looser and stricter four-line tetrameter–trimeter stanzas "ballad stanzas." Wordsworth's "A Slumber Did My Spirit Seal" (1800) is written in the stricter ballad stanza about a loved person who has died and become part of the earth's daily course:

```
A slumber did my spirit seal;
o   B  o   b   o   B o   B
   I had no human fears:
   o  B  o  B o   B    [B]
She seemed a thing that could not feel
  o  B     o  B    o  B    o   B
   The touch of earthly years.
    o  B   o  B    o  B    [B]

No motion has she now, no force;                    5
 O  B  o   B    o  B    O  B
   She neither hears nor sees;
    o  B   o   B    o   B   [B]
Rolled round in earth's diurnal course
 O      B   o  B        oB  o   B
   With rocks, and stones, and trees.
    o    B    o    B    o    B    [B]
```

You may find you want to perform that last line with long pauses between the phrases; to do this in no way disrupts the meter, which is simply suspended through the pauses.

blank verse Unrhymed iambic pentameter. In Chapter 4 we encountered examples from Milton's *Paradise Lost* and from a poem by Mary Jo Salter. Here are two further passages using this common verse form. First, several much-varied lines (130 to 139) from Book One of Wordsworth's *Prelude*, where the poet recounts his feelings when, as a boy, he clung to a mountain cliff trying to reach a raven's nest; and then less agitated, down-to-earth lines (183 to 189) from Book Five of Elizabeth Barrett Browning's novel in verse, *Aurora Leigh*, as she describes how poets should write of their own times.

. . . Oh! when I have hung   130
  B   o B o   B
         b

Above the raven's nest, by knots of grass
o B   o B o   B   o B o   B
  b

And half-inch fissures in the slippery rock
o   B   O   B o   b   o   B   o B
                  B -o- B

But ill sustained, and almost (so it seemed)
 o B   o B   o B o   b o B

Suspended by the blast that blew amain,
 o B o b   o B   o   B o B

Shouldering the naked crag, oh, at that time   135
  B   -o-   B o   B[o]B -o-   B
                               -o=

While on the perilous ridge I hung alone,
  B   -o-   B -o-   B   o B   o B
  o   b   o

With what strange utterance did the loud dry wind
 o   B   O   B   o   b   o B   O B
              B -o-   b

Blow through my ear! the sky seemed not a sky
 B   -o-   B   o B o   B o B
                      Bô B   =o-

Of earth — and with what motion moved the clouds!
o B   -o-   B ô B o   B   o   B

        . . . But poets should
         o   Bo   b

Exert a double vision; should have eyes
o B o B o B o   b   o   B

To see near things as comprehensively   185
  o B   O   B   o   B o B o b

```
As if afar they took their point of sight,
o  b  oB    o  B    o   B    o  B

And distant things as intimately deep
o    B o    B   o B  o b   o B

As if they touched them. Let us strive for this.
o  b   o  B      o    B o   B    o   B

I do distrust the poet who discerns
o  b  o   B   o Bo    b  o B

No character of glory in his times. . .
 O   B o b  o    B o b   o  B
                  -o-   B ô B
```

common measure or **common meter**   See "ballad stanza."

couplet   Two rhyming lines written in the same meter. The following examples are from poems by Anne Bradstreet, the first recognized poet of the English colonies in America. The six lines of iambic tetrameter, in couplets, are the beginning of her poem "Here Follows Some Verses upon the Burning of Our House July 10th, 1666"; these are followed by iambic pentameter couplets from "A Letter to Her Husband, Absent upon Public Employment." This poem is a lament that her husband has had to leave their home to fulfill governmental duties. (A "magazine" is a storehouse.) You will notice that, conforming to the taste of her day, her iambic lines are very regular – "piteous" was no doubt pronounced as a two-syllable word, and "stayest" as a single syllable.

```
In silent night when rest I took
o   B o    B      o   B   o B

For sorrow near I did not look
 o   B o   B  o B   o   B

I wakened was with thund'ring noise
o B o    b   o    B    o    B

And piteous shrieks of dreadful voice.
o    B o      B   o   B   o  B

That fearful sound of "Fire!" and "Fire!"      5
  o    B  o    B   o   B    o    B
```

```
Let no man know is my desire.
o  B   o   B  o  B  oB


My head, my heart, mine eyes, my life, nay, more,
 o  B    o B     o  B    o B    O   B

My joy, my magazine of earthly store,
 o  B   o B o b  o  B    o   B

If two be one, as surely thou and I,
o  B  o B   o  B   o  B  o  B

How stayest thou there, whilst I at Ipswich lie?
 o    B     o   B     o    B o B  o   B
```

end-stopped lines Lines of verse that end with the completion of
   a logical or grammatical unit; the lines by Alexander Pope in
   Chapter 4 are end-stopped iambic pentameter couplets:

> True ease in writing comes from art, not chance,
> As those move easiest who have learn'd to dance.
> 'Tis not enough no harshness gives offence;
> The sound must seem an echo to the sense.

enjambment The carrying of meaning from one line of verse to
   the next without a logical or grammatical break. See "run-on
   lines."

free verse Verse not organized in fixed metrical patterns; also called
   "open form." Most free verse lacks rhyme.

heroic couplet A couplet written in iambic pentameter. ("Heroic"
   is the equivalent of "epic"; late seventeenth-century poets in
   England adopted this meter for their epic poetry and heroic
   dramas.) Alexander Pope's couplets that illustrate *end-stopped
   lines* are heroic couplets. They are also **closed couplets**, in that
   a complete thought is expressed in the two lines.

quatrain A stanza with four lines of verse.

run-on lines A series of lines of verse in which the thought "runs
   on" from one line to the next without a logical or grammatical
   break. Run-on lines, or "enjambed" lines (to use a term from the
   French), are the opposites of end-stopped lines. The passage of
   blank verse by Wordsworth scanned above begins with a series

of three run-on lines that create a sort of breathlessness that helps express a boy's feeling of elation:

```
            . . . Oh! when I have hung
    Above the raven's nest, by knots of grass
    And half-inch fissures in the slippery rock
    But ill sustained, . . .
```

sonnet Traditionally a fourteen-line poem written in iambic pentameter with one of two rhyme schemes, the English (Shakespearean) or the Italian (Petrarchan). The English rhyme scheme is **ababcdcdefefgg**. The Italian rhyme scheme is **abbaabbacdecde** (or some other pattern for the last six lines, like **cdcdcd**). The strict Italian form does not end in a couplet; however, some writers adopt the English couplet-ending for their otherwise Italian sonnets. Non-traditional sonnets, with novel patterns of meter and rhyme (and sometimes excluding these features) are written by many contemporary poets.

stanza A repeating group of two or more lines of verse whose patterns are the same. Most stanzas written in metrical lines also rhyme.

syllabic verse Verse organized not by meters but solely by syllable count. The form is common in many languages, but although a number of distinguished poets have written syllabic verse in English – their lines arranged in patterns based on the numbers of syllables in them – readers are often unaware of this structure and take the poems to be written in free verse. This is because the poems lack the beats and offbeats that create audible and "feelable" rhythm.

It should be noticed that in a different way most of the metrical verse discussed in this book is "syllabic": the metrical lines in a given poem have about the same number of syllables in each line. Or, if the lines in a series of identical stanzas have differing lengths, the poems have the same number of syllables in matching lines. Thus an iambic tetrameter line will usually have eight syllables; an anapestic tetrameter line, twelve; an iambic pentameter line, ten. However, the syllable count may, within limits, vary. For example, iambic pentameter lines can usually vary between nine and twelve syllables before they risk losing the sense of their meter – if the patterns of emphasis conform to the beat-offbeat rule.

tercet   A three-line stanza. A famous use of tercets with interlocking rhymes (**aba bcb cdc ded**, . . .) is Dante's *Divine Comedy*, the great fourteenth-century Italian dream-poem. This particular tercet form is called *terza rima*, Italian for "third rhyme."

verse paragraph   A number of lines grouped not by a fixed pattern but according to content. Very often long poems in blank verse are sectioned into verse paragraphs whose beginning lines are indicated, as in prose, by indentation. The lines from Wordsworth's *Prelude* we scanned earlier (under **blank verse**) conclude a verse paragraph; then the next verse paragraph begins.

```
With what strange utterance did the loud dry wind
Blow through my ear! the sky seemed not a sky
Of earth – and with what motion moved the clouds!
   Dust as we are, the immortal spirit grows
Like harmony in music; . . .
```

METER AND MEANING 7

For six chapters now, we have been exploring the experience of meter and rhythm in a range of poems. This seventh chapter will provide still further practice in using beat prosody, with suggested performances available for comparison. But it will also provide an opportunity to share our experiences of several more poems whose meanings are reinforced by particular rhythms – or in some instances made more complex by them.

The poems we've chosen to discuss have often been written about, some at great length. And many fascinating details about the probable significance of specific images or poetic devices other than meter – all useful for gaining the fullest sense of what may be going on in a poem – are not mentioned here. Certainly, not everyone will agree with our notions about the following poems, and we won't attempt to persuade you that our opinion of what's going on is truer than another's. But we will try to give further suggestions about how any careful reader can assemble evidence to support a point of view by taking meter more fully into account than has been usual.

Several of the discussions are fairly lengthy and detailed, so you may wish to pick and choose among them or consider them one by one at leisure. A speed-read is no doubt possible, but it's not recommended.

In these pages we have often repeated that to understand rhythms in poetry you have to get physical with poems, mouthing and feeling them. And we've seen that meanings do emerge with this physical approach. So in the following exercises and examples, with their commentaries, we will pay even more particular attention to these physicalities, and to how beat scansion can help us understand their workings.

After the initial presentation and discussion of each poem, there will be a "work break" – a break in the argument indicated by a line of asterisks (* * * *). Following that will be our scanned performance of the poem and further commentary. Both the performance and the commentary will be easier to understand if, indeed, you take a break from reading and do the copying, reading aloud, and scanning that will *really* get you into the poem.

THREE SHORTER-LINE-LENGTH POEMS

We start with a poem written in unusually short lines by Langston Hughes, a celebrated member of the group of writers who contributed to the Harlem Renaissance (the flowering of the arts in this predominantly black section of Manhattan in the 1920s and 30s). In "Dream Variations," Hughes contrasts his dream of liberation with an unspecified but easily imagined reality. Like our earliest rhyming verse, "We won't talk of stress," this poem is plainly a two-beat, dimeter one, where double offbeats contribute to a sense of motion and freedom that make it attractive and moving (at least for us). Copy the poem out, read it aloud, and then scan it. Do you think Hughes's choice of this meter – which we hear as basically anapestic, though not in every line – contributes to the effectiveness of what he has to say?

```
To fling my arms wide
In some place of the sun,
To whirl and to dance
Till the white day is done.
Then rest at cool evening                    5
Beneath a tall tree
While night comes on gently.
    Dark like me –
That is my dream!

To fling my arms wide                        10
In the face of the sun,
Dance! Whirl! Whirl!
Till the quick day is done.
Rest at pale evening . . .
```

```
A tall, slim tree . . .                                          15
Night coming tenderly
  Black like me.
```

* * * *

"Dream Variations" is scanned this way in our performance:

```
To fling my arms wide
 o  B    -o=      B
In some place of the sun,
 -o-      B    -o-    B
To whirl and to dance
 o  B      -o-  B
Till the white day is done.
  -o-      B     =o-    B
Then rest at cool evening                                         5
  o  B    -o=     B    o
Beneath a tall tree
 o B    -o=       B
While night comes on gently.
  o      B        -o-  B   o
  Dark like me —
    B   o    B
That is my dream!
  B    -o-     B

To fling my arms wide                                            10
  o  B    -o=      B
In the face of the sun,
 -o-   B    -o-      B
Dance! Whirl! Whirl!
  B        O      B
Till the quick day is done.
  -o-      B      =o-    B
Rest at pale evening . . .
  B    -o=     B    o
```

```
A tall, slim tree . . .                              15
o  B       O    B
Night coming tenderly
  B      -o-    B  -o-
   Black like me.
      B    o   B
```

When thinking about whether Hughes's choice of a meter that is basically but not entirely anapestic dimeter contributes to the poem's effectiveness, you probably guessed our answer. It seems to us that the lack of strict metrical regularity within a strongly rhythmical poem allows the poet to achieve wonderful effects of contrast. (This metrical practice is often found in Hughes's poems more specifically modeled on popular blues rhythms.) The principal metrical contrast – which we can hear in this performance and see in the scansion – is between the easy, light flow of the lines with the double offbeats and the sterner lines without them.

The first stanza, for example, has only one line without a double offbeat – "Dark like me" – which follows the more gracious "While night comes on gently." For us this creates a striking and sorrowful comparison, in both meter and image, between the loveliness of a world where one can whirl and dance as night draws on, and the poet's "real" world where being black is not always lovely, and where by many his "darkness" is disdained.

The same effect is created by the same means at the end of the second stanza, with the even stronger statement, "Black like me." But in this stanza there are two other lines without double offbeats: "Dance! Whirl! Whirl!" and "A tall, slim tree." What of these lines?

The first is very strong – so strong, in fact, that in a metrical context other than dimeter the line would probably be heard as trimeter stress verse, with virtual offbeats – like Tennyson's "Break, break, break." We've called the first "Whirl!" an emphasized offbeat, an **O** between two **B**'s; but perhaps you will feel it's more than that. Hughes seems to be pushing the verse to the limit of the meter, almost breaking out of it with the force of the words and the actions they describe. So indeed this line's *metrical* strength expresses the very kind of energy which has the potential to realize dreams in the everyday world.

Then, the second no-double-offbeat line creates a moment in the poem when the poet almost becomes that "tall, slim tree."

Although here the grammatical form of the line, with its absence of notable pauses, allows us to experience it as a smoother one than "Dance! Whirl! Whirl!," its firm emphases on the three words "tall," "slim," and "tree" carry the promise that dreams may, with strength and energy, be fulfilled.

Another well-known poem, William Blake's "The Tyger" (printed and illustrated by the poet in his *Songs of Experience* of 1794), has a particular metrical feature that merits attention. The poem unmistakably has four beats, so it is a tetrameter poem. But what kind of tetrameter poem? Perform its opening stanza yourself (you may well be familiar with these lines) and feel the beats:

```
Tyger! Tyger! burning bright
In the forests of the night,
What immortal hand or eye
Could frame thy fearful symmetry?
```

First: have you experienced the "Tyger! Tyger! burning bright" rhythm before? Perhaps when you were very young? How about in nursery rhymes, like "Rain, rain, go away"? Or "Jack, be nimble, Jack, be quick"? If these verses were a part of your childhood, you probably remember the second lines: "Come again another day," and "Jack, jump over the candlestick." In such nursery rhymes, if the first word in a line gets an emphasis, the first word in the following line is likely to be emphasized too – whether it would be in normal speech or not. Another familiar nursery rhyme (written a few years after Blake's poem) shows this tendency, and matches the rhythm of the first lines of "The Tyger" perfectly: "Twinkle, twinkle, little star, /How I wonder what you are."

If you hear, as we do, a nursery rhyme pattern underlying "Tyger! Tyger! burning bright," you will probably emphasize the "In" that begins the second line. If the poem had a subtler, non-nursery-rhyme rhythm, the "In" would almost certainly be unemphasized, a small **b**. Or it might even be felt as part of a double offbeat at the start of a *three*-beat line – for example, "The creature had been stirring/ In the forests of the night," which would probably be read: "The **crea**ture **had** been **stir**ring/In the **for**ests **of** the **night**." But if the nursery-rhyme rhythm is recollected when we perform Blake's opening lines, we will give the "In" (and perhaps the "of" as well) the strong emphasis of the childhood meter – even though the questions Blake asks in his poem are hardly children's questions.

In the previous chapter we mentioned that a standard *trochaic tetrameter* line begins with a beat, has four beats with offbeats between them, and ends with an offbeat. Blake's poem begins, then, in a trochaic manner, and although there is no offbeat at the end of the line, this absence, as we have noted, occurs frequently in trochaic verse. But the last line of the stanza, if taken by itself, is *iambic tetrameter*, because it has an initial offbeat. In the simpler terms of beat prosody, we would say that these are all four-beat duple lines ending on a beat, but some begin on a beat and some on an offbeat. What is there to say about this peculiar metrical situation where there are *two* kinds of line, which we can call trochaic and iambic? What meaning is created by their use?

We'll give our answers to these questions once you've had a chance to come to your own conclusions about the poem as a whole. So copy out the complete poem, perform it, and scan it.

By the way, do you think (as we do) that by using a spelling of "tiger" that was becoming old-fashioned even when the poet wrote, the "tyger" is made more mysterious than a tiger – or whatever this tiger might stand for – would be? Another point: you will note that to accommodate his meter, Blake asks us to treat the word "fire" as a two-syllable word in line 6 and as a one-syllable word in line 8. (As we've seen, many English words have such a choice of pronunciations.)

```
Tyger! Tyger! burning bright
In the forests of the night,
What immortal hand or eye
Could frame thy fearful symmetry?

In what distant deeps or skies               5
Burnt the fire of thine eyes?
On what wings dare he aspire?
What the hand dare seize the fire?

And what shoulder, and what art,
Could twist the sinews of thy heart?         10
And when thy heart began to beat,
What dread hand? and what dread feet?
```

```
What the hammer? what the chain?
In what furnace was thy brain?
What the anvil? what dread grasp                    15
Dare its deadly terrors clasp?

When the stars threw down their spears,
And watered heaven with their tears,
Did He smile his work to see?
Did he who made the Lamb make thee?                 20

Tyger! Tyger! burning bright
In the forests of the night,
What immortal hand or eye
Dare frame thy fearful symmetry?
```

* * * *

Here is our performance of the poem, emphasizing the first syllable of each line that begins with a beat – lines we're calling trochaic. If you've preferred unemphasized **b**'s for "In" (in lines 2, 5, 14 and 22), "On" (in line 7), and "And" (in line 9), that's okay too.

```
Tyger! Tyger! burning bright
 B o   B o   B o    B

In the forests of the night,
B   o B o   b   o B

What immortal hand or eye
  B o B o   B   o B

Could frame thy fearful symmetry? (x)
 o      B   o B o   B o b

In what distant deeps or skies                      5
B   o  B o   B   o    B

Burnt the fire of thine eyes?
 B      o B o b    o   B

On what wings dare he aspire?
B   o   B    0    B o B
         B   ô B   -o-   B

What the hand dare seize the fire?
  B   o B   0   B     o B
```

And what shoulder, and what art,
B   o   B   o   b   o B

Could twist the sinews of thy heart? (x)   10
 o   B   o B o   b   o B

And when thy heart began to beat, (x)
o   B   o B   o B   o B

What dread hand? and what dread feet?
 B   O   B   o   B   O   B

What the hammer? what the chain?
 B   o B o   B   o   B

In what furnace was thy brain?
B   o   B   o   b   o   B

What the anvil? what dread grasp   15
 B   o B o   B   O   B

Dare its deadly terrors clasp?
 B   o   B   o B o   B

When the stars threw down their spears,
 B   o   B   O   B   o   B

And watered heaven with their tears, (x)
o   B o   B o   b   o   B

Did he smile his work to see?
 B   o   B   o   B   o B

Did he who made the Lamb make thee? (x)   20
 o   B o   B   o B   O   B

Tyger! Tyger! burning bright
 B o   B o   B o   B

In the forests of the night,
B   o   B o   b   o B

What immortal hand or eye
 B o B o   B o B

Dare frame thy fearful symmetry? (x)
 O   B   o B o   B o   b

Having done our scansion, it's easy to separate out the iambic lines from the trochaic ones which clearly predominate – eighteen out of twenty-four. (We've put an (x) beside the six iambic lines so they can be spotted readily.) First, is there a different *feel* to the two types of lines?

You will have your opinions, and these are ours. The iambic lines are less rugged, gentler; whereas the trochaic lines are almost harshly emphatic. And in a physical way this difference makes what is being said more meaningful.

The trochaic lines refer to the non-human, or to ominously detached *parts* of the human body, or to things beyond-the-human: "forest of the night," "immortal hand or eye," "distant deeps or skies," "hammer," "chain," "furnace," "shoulder," "dread grasp" – all that provokes awe and terror.

To what do the iambic lines refer? Here they are as a group:

```
Could frame thy fearful symmetry? (4)

Could twist the sinews of thy heart? (10)

And when thy heart began to beat, (11)

And watered heaven with their tears, (18)

Did he who made the Lamb make thee? (20)

Dare frame thy fearful symmetry? (24)
```

For us, these gentler lines bring reminders of a more human world into the poem in these ways:

10 and 11: Passing over line 4 for a moment, notice that lines 10 and 11 concern not hand, eye, foot, or shoulder, but the beating heart, the source of life.

18: Stars watering heaven "with their tears" recollect human weeping.

20: The line recalls the mildness of the Lamb (which suggests possible human goodness and spiritual gentleness).

4 and 24: Though these lines express fear and awe, they are the only lines in the poem which end with *unemphasized* beats (**sym**-me-**try**). This softening of the stern meter suggests the possibility of some kind of reconciliation between frail human beings and the mysterious, often terrifying natural and spiritual worlds in which

they live. And the *emphasized offbeat*, "Dare," that begins the final line suggests, by its very forcefulness as it pushes against the metrical pattern, that humans may themselves have the power to endure, even challenge, these mysteries and terrors.

So the iambic lines give us, because of their more regular meter, images that are *felt* differently from the images created in the trochaic lines, giving the poem as a whole a wider range of emotions to which the reader and performer can respond.

Did Blake consciously plot the irregular occurrence of these gentler lines amid the sterner ones? Was it calculated? Or in the writing of the poem – in the emotionally involving moments when the poem was forming in his mind – did two feelings possess him: first, awe at the grandeur and terror of aspects of the world (coupled, many people feel, with awe at the power of the artist's own imagination); but second, and at the same time, a sympathetic sense of the fragility of human beings in a stern and mysterious cosmos?

Now a poem in iambic trimeter. The poem is about a young boy "waltzing" with his father, so trimeter is a logical choice, since a waltz is a dance in a flowing one-two-three meter. But as a performance will let you hear, and a scansion will let you see, this waltz is far from smooth. (The virtual beats you may feel at the end of the lines also contribute to a sense of haltingness and unease – although the absence of any four-beat lines means that there is a somewhat weaker expectation for a fourth beat than is the case with ballad stanzas.) The poem is the twentieth-century American poet Theodore Roethke's "My Papa's Waltz," first published in 1948. How does metrical variation enhance the vividness of particular events in the poem?

```
The whiskey on your breath
Could make a small boy dizzy;
But I hung on like death:
Such waltzing was not easy.

We romped until the pans                          5
Slid from the kitchen shelf;
My mother's countenance
Could not unfrown itself.
```

```
The hand that held my wrist
Was battered on one knuckle;                              10
At every step you missed
My right ear scraped a buckle.

You beat time on my head
With a palm caked hard by dirt,
Then waltzed me off to bed                               15
Still clinging to your shirt.
```

* * * *

Omitting virtual beat symbols, here is our performance:

```
The whiskey on your breath
  o   B  o   b   o     B
Could make a small boy dizzy;
  o     B  o   B    O   B  o
But I hung on like death:
  o B  O   B   o     B
Such waltzing was not easy.
  O    B      -o-    B ôB  o
        B   o   b   o B


We romped until the pans                                  5
  o B      o  b    o  B
Slid from the kitchen shelf;
   B    -o-    B   o     B
My mother's countenance
  o B  o     B   o b
Could not unfrown itself.
  o     B  o   B   o  B


The hand that held my wrist
  o  B     o   B    o   B
Was battered on one knuckle;                             10
  o   B      -o-  B  ô  B   o
```

```
At every step you missed
o  B o     B   o  B

My right ear scraped a buckle.
o   B    O      B    o B   o

You beat time on my head
 o   B  ô B   -o-   B

With a palm caked hard by dirt,
  -o-  B    O      B    o  B

Then waltzed me off to bed          15
  o    B      o B   o  B

Still clinging to your shirt.
   O     B  o    b  o    B
```

Did you discover points in the poem where meter and metrical variation enhance the vividness of particular events? Here are several that seem unusually prominent and successful to us. We'll list them by lines:

2: After the first regular line, the extra offbeat at the end of line two enhances the sense of dizziness, while the unexpected emphasis on "boy" gives three strong thumps together, increasing the sense of tension in the scene.

4: In our preferred performance, the double and implied offbeats producing the -o- **B** ô **B** figure, and then the extra offbeat at the end, make the line as *uneasy* as the situation that the words are picturing. A more regular performance (perhaps with emphasis on "was") gives prominence to the *difficulty* of the "romp."

6: The double offbeat "from the" between the initial beat on "slid" and the second beat on "kit-" – the only time in the poem that this common rhythmic figure, initial inversion, occurs – gives a sense of sliding from the first beat to the second, creating an aural equivalent of the image we can visualize.

10: This line uses the same rhythmic figure as line 4, the double offbeat followed by two beats with an implied offbeat between them; here it causes, for us, the tame "-ered on" followed by **"one knuck-"** to sound like the battering that caused the father's injury (which perhaps suggests how hardworking he is).

12: The three emphasized words in the phrase "right ear scraped" – the **B O B** figure – help convey a sense of the force of the action. Note too that all of the words in this line require a lot of tongue, jaw, and lip work – particularly the word "scraped."

13 and 14: Both of these lines, with their *three* kinds of offbeat (double, emphasized, and implied), continue the sense of agitation and near-violence. The side-by-side stressed beats on "beat time," separated only by an implied offbeat, enact what they state. The poet seems to be pulling out all the stops before his final concluding lines.

15 and 16: The regularity of these lines, after all of the tumult in so many of the earlier ones, suggests a harmony and reconcilement at the end of the "waltz," where the boy clings to his father's shirt as he is waltzed, not dragged, to bed. The last line seems to reinforce metrically what the image of clinging has suggested. First there is strength at the line's beginning with the two emphasized words, "**still cling**ing." Then, with the second beat unemphasized, at the conclusion of the line – and the poem – there is calm.

Roethke, by his skillful control of meter and variations on its expected pattern, makes vivid not only the details he describes, but the complexity of emotions at work in a family scene being recollected in all of its intensity.

TWO LONGER-LINE-LENGTH POEMS

In the earlier chapters of this book we devoted considerable attention to five-beat lines, so from the vast number of possible choices we will look at only two further examples: another sonnet by Shakespeare, where the complexities of his five-beat lines serve less to *reinforce* what the words are saying than to *challenge* or even *contradict* them; and a poem by the contemporary poet Adrienne Rich, where loose and strict pentameter lines convey their own messages about what life is like for the poem's central figure.

Our Shakespeare sonnet is one of his most famous: number 116, which begins, "Let me not to the marriage of true minds/Admit impediments," and makes a memorable claim that love can be absolutely constant and unchanging.

Here is the sonnet for your performance and scansion. We're quite certain that you will discover when reading aloud that the poet's claims about love's constancy are very urgently, very forcefully stated – this is not a gentle poem. After completing the scansion it will be clear that entirely regular iambic pentameter lines are rare; that there are many emphasized O's and double offbeats where one part is emphasized (-o= or =o-); and that there are numerous implied or virtual offbeats between two adjacent strong beats. A line from Shakespeare's *Hamlet* which over time has become proverbial is "The lady doth protest too much, methinks." Are the statements about love's constancy over-done? What do your performance and your scansion tell you?

```
Let me not to the marriage of true minds
Admit impediments; love is not love
Which alters when it alteration finds,
Or bends with the remover to remove.
O no, it is an ever fixèd mark                     5
That looks on tempests and is never shaken;
It is the star to every wandering bark,
Whose worth's unknown, although his height be taken.
Love's not Time's fool, though rosy lips and cheeks
Within his bending sickle's compass come;          10
Love alters not with his brief hours and weeks,
But bears it out even to the edge of doom.
    If this be error and upon me proved,
    I never writ, nor no man ever loved.
```

* * * *

For Shakespeare's sonnet 116 many alternative ways of scanning specific lines are possible, and in our scansion we've shown only a few of them. But it's not likely that an untroubled scansion will emerge from any energetic reading. Though all of the lines have their five beats (Shakespeare will fulfill his reader's expectations in this regard), and though here and there quite regular lines appear (for example: 3, 7, 10, 13, and 14), most lines have notable differences; and some are very complex indeed, with several possibilities of performance. (Note that the word "even," in line 12, was usually pronounced as a monosyllable in Shakespeare's time.)

Let me not to the marriage of true minds
 B o B -o-   B   -o-   B ô B

Admit impediments; love is not love
o B o B -o-   B o B ô B

Which alters when it alteration finds,
  o   B o   b o b o B o B

Or bends with the remover to remove.
o B ô B   -o- B o   b o B
   B   o   b o B

O no, it is an ever fixèd mark   5
O B[o]B -o- B o B o   B
  B o b o

That looks on tempests and is never shaken;
  o   B   o B o   b o   B o   B o

It is the star to every wandering bark,
o b   o B   o B o B   o   B
B -o-   B

Whose worth's unknown, although his height be taken.
  o   B   o   B   o b   o   B   o B o

Love's not Time's fool, though rosy lips and cheeks
 B   =o=   B   o   B o B o   B
 O   B   O   B

Within his bending sickle's compass come;   10
 o B o B o   B o   B o   B

Love alters not with his brief hours and weeks,
 O B o   B   o   B   O   B   o   B
       B   -o-   B ô B

But bears it out even to the edge of doom.
 o   B   o B ôB   -o-   B   o   B

  If this be error and upon me proved,
  o   B   oB o b   oB o   B

  I never writ, nor no man ever loved.
  o B o   B   o   B O B o   B

The scansion demonstrates what the performance causes us to feel
from the start, where the opening two lines plainly create a mood of

agitation and anxiety, as if the poet is telling himself not to think the unthinkable – that true love is only a dream. Further, one can observe that the metrically regular third line (and, possibly, the fourth) is weakly stated, with a predominance of unstressed syllables, suggesting that even here entire confidence is lacking. And the agitation continues. In quite-even lines like six and eight – lines asserting that love cannot be shaken, that its true worth surpasses measurement – lack of firmness can be felt when the extra offbeat at the end of the line is encountered. (These are the only two "offbeat endings" in the poem.)

The tensions remain evident, as the scansion demonstrates, until at the concluding couplet we seem to achieve a calm statement of conviction in quite-regular iambic pentameter. But after the metrical difficulties we have gone through to get to it, the couplet can seem more like bravado than a statement of a heartfelt certainty. (Compare the effect of an *entirely* regular line: "I never writ and no one ever loved.") Of the eight words in the last line, by the way, three are negatives: never, nor, no.

Now the final poem. When discussing Blake's "The Tyger," we noted how two sorts of tetrameter lines, along with the images in them, produced complex feelings of awe, terror, and gentleness. This chapter's last pentameter example of the contribution made by meter to meaning will return us to a tiger – or, rather, the tigers that a woman is embroidering on a decorative screen.

Adrienne Rich is one of America's most acclaimed contemporary poets and a prominent feminist. Although her later poetry is written principally in free verse, "Aunt Jennifer's Tigers," an earlier poem, uses iambic pentameter couplets with great skill to suggest – even more strongly than what is *said* – the way in which Aunt Jennifer's life is rigidly structured and constrained. Here is the poem for performance and scansion. Which lines have the most strictly regular meter? Which lines have double offbeats, and where? What meanings expressed by the words are strengthened or deepened by metrical variation or lack of variation?

```
Aunt Jennifer's tigers prance across a screen,
Bright topaz denizens of a world of green.
They do not fear the men beneath the tree;
They pace in sleek chivalric certainty.
```

Aunt Jennifer's fingers fluttering through her wool   5
Find even the ivory needle hard to pull.
The massive weight of Uncle's wedding band
Sits heavily upon Aunt Jennifer's hand.

When Aunt is dead, her terrified hands will lie
Still ringed with ordeals she was mastered by.   10
The tigers in the panel that she made
Will go on prancing, proud and unafraid.

* * * *

Here is "Aunt Jennifer's Tigers" as we perform it, with likely alternatives:

```
Aunt Jennifer's tigers prance across a screen,
 o   B  -o-    B o    B   o B   o    B
 O

Bright topaz denizens of a world of green.
  O    B o  B -o-   b  o B    o    B

They do not fear the men beneath the tree;
  B  -o-   B    o B  o b     o  B
  o   B o

They pace in sleek chivalric certainty.
  o   B   o   B     o B o  B   o   b


Aunt Jennifer's fingers fluttering through her wool   5
 o   B  -o-    B o    B -o-     b    o   B
 O

Find even the ivory needle hard to pull.
 O   B  -o-   B -o-  B   o B    o B
               B   o B

The massive weight of Uncle's wedding band
 o B  o    B     o B o    B  o    B

Sits heavily upon Aunt Jennifer's hand.
 O    B  o b o B   o   B  -o-    B
                O

When Aunt is dead, her terrified hands will lie
 o   B   o  B     o  B  -o-   B   o    B
```

```
Still ringed with ordeals she was mastered by.      10
  O     B      o   B o      b  o   B o      B
        B         -o-  B   ô  B
The tigers in the panel that she made
  o  B o    b    o   B o     b    o  B
Will go on prancing, proud and unafraid.
  o     B O     B o       B    o    B o B
```

To begin: which lines have the most strictly regular meter? We'll list them:

```
They do not fear the men beneath the tree; (3)
```

(This may be scanned as regular or not, depending on your performance.)

```
They pace in sleek chivalric certainty. (4)
```

```
The massive weight of Uncle's wedding band (7)
```

```
Still ringed with ordeals she was mastered by. (10)
```

(This may be scanned as regular or not, depending on your performance.)

```
The tigers in the panel that she made (11)
```

```
Will go on prancing, proud and unafraid. (12)
```

What can be said about these six lines? Here's what we'd say: line 3, if given its alternate, regular performance (not our preferred one), suggests a harmonious world where men are not to be feared; line 4 tells of the tigers' world of steady certainty; line 7 gives the sense of a steady, grim heaviness in Aunt Jennifer's marriage which, like the wedding band, encircles her; line 10 – if read with regular **B**'s and **o**'s – expresses the steadiness of the unrelenting ordeals that mastered her in her marriage; and the concluding lines 11 and 12 tell of the strong, rhythmical and beautiful "other" world which Aunt Jennifer has created in her embroidery, but which belongs not to her but to the tigers of her imagination.

How, then, would we sum up the meanings of the *regular* lines? By saying that the steady rhythms emphasize two strong but different feelings: in those lines that speak of the wedding ring and the ordeals, the meter heightens feelings of constraint; and in the lines describing the tigers in their luminous world, the meter heightens a sense of confident and secure freedom.

And what of the *less-regular* lines which have the double offbeats? First, we can make a general statement: because of the double offbeat in her name, "Aunt Jennifer" seems more fragile and tentative than strong, and so all of the lines in which her name appears contrast with the lines that convey strength. (How would the poem be changed if "Aunt Jennifer" were "Aunt Susan"?) But there are other moments in the meter when by their rhythm the double offbeats convey a sense of fragility.

```
Aunt Jennifer's tigers prance across a screen, (1)

Bright topaz denizens of a world of green. (2)

They do not fear the men beneath the tree; (3)

Aunt Jennifer's fingers fluttering through her wool (5)

Find even the ivory needle hard to pull. (6)

Sits heavily upon Aunt Jennifer's hand. (8)

When Aunt is dead, her terrified hands will lie (9)

Still ringed with ordeals she was mastered by. (10)
```

Line 1 conveys fragility through the Aunt's name itself. Line 3, if heard as in our preferred performance (**they** do not **fear**), conveys Aunt Jennifer's fragility by contrasting "her" with "they" – the tigers who are not afraid of men. Line 5 adds to the sense of Aunt Jennifer's fragility by having her fingers "flut-ter-ing" (remember Wordsworth's daffodils). The double offbeats (we hear two in our preferred performance) weaken the alternating rhythm of line 6, as though Aunt Jennifer lacks strength even to pull a needle through cloth. Then in line 9 Aunt Jennifer's hands are "ter-ri-fied." And in line 10, if given the alternate performance (**ringed** with or**deals she**), the still greater complexity of rhythm – with the double offbeat–implied offbeat rhythmic figure – gives not a sense of the "steadiness of the unrelenting ordeals that mastered her in her marriage," as above, but of the immensity and overpoweringness of the ordeals faced by this fragile woman.

So where the metrically regular lines have represented strength, these rhythmically more-complex lines convey, on the whole, fragility.

But wait. What about line 2?

```
Bright topaz denizens of a world of green.
  O     B o  B -o-  b o B   o   B
```

Here we have another line with a double offbeat; shouldn't it also represent fragility?

Well, what's different about this situation? Notice that the line's first word, "Bright," must be emphasized, and so with "**Bright to**paz" the line begins very strongly. Having, therefore, established a sense of strength, our poet can add, with the double offbeat, a feeling not of fragility but of mysteriousness by use of the word "denizens," which simply means "inhabitants," but which is so unusual in ordinary talk that it can suggest, along with topaz and tigers, every exotic thing which is absent from Aunt Jennifer's life. Here, then, the meaning of a single word – *denizens* – is strengthened and deepened by its unexpected metrical contour.

IDENTIFYING METERS AND STANZA-FORMS

8

Here are thirteen short poems and excerpts from poems, written from the sixteenth century to the present. Perform them, sense the patterns that the beats and offbeats create, and put the conventional labels on them – first the predominant-meter and line-length labels for the rhythms, and then the form or stanza labels. The labels we would use are listed at the end of the exercise, with a few comments about occasional metrical surprises and several extended discussions.

1. From Christopher Marlowe's "The Passionate Shepherd to His Love" (1599)

> Come live with me, and be my love,
> And we will all the pleasures prove*
> That valleys, groves, hills and fields,
> Woods, or sleepy mountain yields.
>
> And we will sit upon the rocks,   5
> Seeing the shepherds feed their flocks
> By shallow rivers, to whose falls
> Melodious birds sing madrigals. . . .
>
> *prove: try out

2. From the song "Fear No More" in Shakespeare's play *Cymbeline* (1609)

> Fear no more the heat o' th' sun,*
>   Nor the furious winter's rages;

Thou thy worldly task hast done,
   Home art gone, and ta'en thy wages.*
Golden lads and girls all must,   5
As chimney sweepers, come to dust.

* o' th' sun: of the sun; ta'en thy wages: taken your wages

3. From Andrew Marvell's "To His Coy Mistress" (1681)

Had we but world enough, and time,
This coyness, Lady, were no crime.
We would sit down, and think which way
To walk, and pass our long love's day. . . .
   But at my back I always hear   5
Time's winged chariot hurrying near;
And yonder all before us lie
Deserts of vast eternity.

4. Phyllis Wheatley's "On Being Brought from Africa to America"
   (1773)

'Twas mercy brought me from my pagan land,
Taught my benighted soul to understand
That there's a God, that there's a Saviour too:
Once I redemption neither sought nor knew.
Some view that sable race with scornful eye: 5
"Their color is a diabolic dye."
Remember, Christians, Negroes black as Cain
May be refined and join the angelic strain.

5. From Samuel Taylor Coleridge's "The Rime of the Ancient
   Mariner" (1798)

All in a hot and copper sky,
The bloody Sun, at noon,
Right up above the mast did stand,
No bigger than the Moon.

Day after day; day after day,   5
We stuck, nor breath nor motion;

As idle as a painted ship
Upon a painted ocean.

Water, water, every where,
And all the boards did shrink;   10
Water, water, every where
Nor any drop to drink.

6. The third, final stanza of John Keats's "To Autumn" (1819)

Where are the songs of spring? Ay, where are they?
   Think not of them, thou hast thy music too, —
While barred clouds bloom the soft-dying day,
   And touch the stubble-plains with rosy hue;
Then in a wailful choir the small gnats mourn   5
   Among the river sallows,* borne aloft
      Or sinking as the light wind lives or dies;
And full-grown lambs loud bleat from hilly bourne;*
   Hedge-crickets sing; and now with treble soft
   The red-breast whistles from a garden-croft;*   10
      And gathering swallows twitter in the skies.

*sallows: willows [6]; bourne: place *or* realm [8]; croft: a small plot of
ground

7. The first of the four sections of Matthew Arnold's "Dover Beach"
   (1861)

The sea is calm to-night.
The tide is full, the moon lies fair
Upon the straits; — on the French coast the light
Gleams and is gone; the cliffs of England stand,
Glimmering and vast, out in the tranquil bay.   5
Come to the window, sweet is the night-air!
Only, from the long line of spray
Where the sea meets the moon-blanch'd land,
Listen! you hear the grating roar
Of pebbles which the waves draw back, and fling,   10
At their return, up the high strand,
Begin, and cease, and then again begin,

```
With tremulous cadence slow, and bring
The eternal note of sadness in.
```

8. Gerard Manley Hopkins's "Spring and Fall: to a young child"
(1880)

In autograph manuscripts sent to two of his friends, the poet supplied
all of the accents and the single italicized word we reproduce here –
as a guide, and as a clear illustration of one poet's concern that his
work in unusual rhythmic patterns be heard and performed as he
would wish. Giving emphasis to the syllables Hopkins marks, you
will hear a familiar rhythm, but a rhythm with metrical innovations
that contribute to what strikes us as a remarkably anguished, resigned,
yet kindly speaking voice.

Notice Hopkins's verbal inventions: is it hard to figure out what
words like "Goldengrove," "wanwood," and "leafmeal" probably
mean? (Likely definitions are given in the comments.) "Ghost" seems
to be Margaret's soul, though it may be every person's.

```
Márgarét, áre you gríeving
Over Goldengrove unleaving?
Leáves, líke the thíngs of mán, you
With your fresh thoughts care for, can you?
Áh! ás the héart grows ólder                    5
It will come to such sights colder
By and by, nor spare a sigh
Though worlds of wanwood leafmeal lie;
And yet you will weep and know why.
Now no matter, child, the name:                 10
Sórrow's spríngs áre the sáme.
Nor mouth had, no nor mind, expressed
What héart héard of, ghóst guéssed:
It ís the blíght mán was bórn for,
It is Margaret you mourn for.                    15
```

9. The first stanza of Thomas Hardy's "Thoughts of Phena" (1890)

The poem was written on receiving news of the death of a woman to
whom two decades earlier the poet had been engaged.

Not a line of her writing have I,
    Not a thread of her hair,
No mark of her late time as dame in her dwelling,
                                    whereby
    I may picture her there;
    And in vain do I urge my unsight   5
        To conceive my lost prize
At her close whom I knew when her dreams were
                        upbrimming with light,
        And with laughter her eyes.

10. Section four of T. S. Eliot's "Burnt Norton" (1936)

Time and the bell have buried the day,
The black cloud carries the sun away.
Will the sunflower turn to us, will the clematis
Stray down, bend to us; tendril and spray
Clutch and cling?   5
Chill
Fingers of yew be curled
Down on us? After the kingfisher's wing
Has answered light to light, and is silent, the
                            light is still
At the still point of the turning world.   10

11. The first two stanzas and the last stanza of Elizabeth Bishop's
    "One Art" (1976)

The art of losing isn't hard to master;
so many things seem filled with the intent
to be lost that their loss is no disaster.

Lose something every day. Accept the fluster
of lost door keys, the hour badly spent.   5
The art of losing isn't hard to master.

    . . .

— Even losing you (the joking voice, a gesture
I love) I shan't have lied. It's evident

```
the art of losing's not too hard to master
though it may look like (Write it!) like disaster.
```

12. John Agard's "Is More Than a Snapshot Mirror" (1982)

This poem is from Agard's collection called "Man to Pan" (a pan is a round drum, hammered out from the lid of a steel oil drum, on which a musical scale can be played). It is an example of dub poetry – a style of performance poetry, usually accompanied by Afro-Caribbean drumming, which originated in Jamaica and became popular in the London suburbs. (The subtitle of the collection is "A Cycle of Poems to be Performed with Drums and Steelpans.")

```
Is more than a snapshot mirror
reflecting panman face
in a mood of concentration
complete with perspiration

Is more than a straw / hat / native              5
making a merry steel show
whilst he catching ass to live
in some bad / john / ghetto

Is more than knocking out a tune
on a sunbeach / package / tour                   10
with rum flowing like blood
and the body calling for more

No/
pan deeper than that man
        is a heap of history in you hand         15
```

13. Paul Muldoon's "The Train" (1998)

This contemporary poet from Northern Ireland – who lives in the United States – structures his sonnets with a freedom that exemplifies the practice of many writers seeking new ways to use traditional forms.

```
I've been trying, my darling, to explain
to myself how it is that some freight train
```

loaded with ballast so a track may rest
easier in its bed should be what's roused

us both from ours, tonight as every night,   5
despite its being miles off and despite
our custom of putting to the very
back of the mind all that's customary

and then, since it takes forever to pass
with its car after car of coal and gas   10
and salt and wheat and rails and railway ties,

how it seems determined to give the lie
to the notion, my darling,
that we, not it, might be the constant thing.

LABELS AND COMMENTS

1. From Christopher Marlowe's "The Passionate Shepherd to His Love."
   Iambic tetrameter stanzas, or quatrains.

After two regular opening lines, there is an unexpected virtual offbeat between "groves" and "hills" in line three. For us the scansion,

```
That valleys, groves, hills and fields,
  o   B  o     B  [o]B   o   B
```

shows the poet creating a feeling of eagerness on the part of the shepherd to heap up the pleasures that he is proposing for his love. A more casual line, "That valleys, groves, and hills, and fields" would seem less urgent. The omission of the expected offbeat at the beginning of line four further enhances this feeling of urgency. Yet the poem retains a song-like lilt, thanks to the tetrameter quatrain's simple and strong meter.

2. From the song "Fear No More" in Shakespeare's play *Cymbeline*.
   Trochaic tetrameter.

The six-line stanza rhyming **ababcc** is often encountered in both tetrameter and pentameter poems. (The last six lines of a Shakespearean sonnet follow this pattern.) A full metrical description of the four-beat lines would note that 1, 3, and 5 begin and end on beats; 2 and 4 begin on beats and end on offbeats; and 6 begins on an offbeat and ends on a beat (that is, it is an *iambic* tetrameter). This kind of freedom at the beginnings and ends of lines is typical of one version of four-beat meter (the most famous example being Milton's pair of poems, *L'Allegro* and *Il Pensoroso*). However, beginning virtually all lines on a beat gives the verse a distinctive chant-like rhythm that is characteristic of trochaic verse, so "trochaic tetrameter" is the best label to use for the overall pattern. In the play, the verse is sung over the (presumed) dead body of the heroine, but even if it is spoken it conveys, with its regular, simple meter and end-stopped lines, a feeling of quiet grief.

3. From Andrew Marvell's "To His Coy Mistress."
   Iambic tetrameter couplets.
   Though in the forty-six-line poem as a whole there are several run-on (enjambed) lines, end-stopped lines predominate. You probably realized in performing these lines that if one keeps the meter regular, the word "winged" in line six will be pronounced as two syllables: "**wing**-éd." An interesting alternative performance could replace the emphasized offbeat on "Time's" with a beat, creating a particularly strong sense of the power of Time: "**Time's** winged **char**iot." This alternative performance would not have been Marvell's, however, as it would reduce the number of syllables in his tetrameter line from eight to seven.
   Notice how much variation Marvell achieves, both to keep the verse supple and interesting and to enhance the meanings and feelings being conveyed. The opening couplet (which is the opening of the poem and of the speaker's attempt to charm the woman he is addressing) is regular and quite relaxed, while the second uses a run-on to evoke something of the imagined stretching of time it describes. In the second set of lines (which come after a much longer evocation of an imagined world), the speaker's urgency is felt in the tension between the meter's demand for an opening offbeat and the emphasis we need to give to "Time's," and in the initial inversion in "Deserts."

4. Phyllis Wheatley's "On Being Brought from Africa to America."
   Iambic pentameter couplets.
   Here America's first published black woman poet, a child prodigy educated by the family that purchased her from a slave ship

in Boston, writes in a conventional eighteenth-century style: quite evenly metered ten-syllable couplets (with a probable elision of "the angelic" to "th' angelic" rather than having a double offbeat – and consequently eleven syllables). The occasional initial inversion ("Taught my. . . ," "Once my. . . ,"), unemphasized beat ("from," "is," "be") and emphasized offbeat ("Some. . .") keep the rhythm flexible.

5. From Samuel Taylor Coleridge's "The Rime of the Ancient Mariner."

Ballad stanzas; alternating iambic tetrameter and trimeter lines, here rhymed **xaxa**.

The strong rhythm of the ballad is felt in the four-beat groupings (including the virtual beats at the ends of alternate lines) that taken together can feel like eight-beat rhymed couplets. There is a notable virtual offbeat in the line "Day after day; day after day." The scansion here,

```
Day after day; day after day,
 B   -o-   B [o]B   -o-   B
```

shows particularly well how the line itself can convey that feeling of monotony and repetitiveness which the stanza as a whole is describing. In the last of the quoted stanzas, Coleridge drops the initial offbeat in the first and third lines (something allowed by the ballad form's lack of strictness about numbers of syllables) to create an instantly memorable incantation.

6. The third, final stanza of John Keats's "To Autumn."

Iambic pentameter, with a full complement of various **B**'s and **b**'s and **o**'s and **O**'s, and a complex rhyme-scheme (**ababcdecdde**).

The word "barred" in the third line is pronounced as a two-syllable word, "barr-éd," so that it fits the meter. We can be sure of this because in other stanzas of the poem Keats shows that the words "mossed" (covered with moss), "reaped," and "drowsed" (made drowsy) should be pronounced as single-syllable words by writing "moss'd," "reap'd," and "drows'd" – in every case making the words fit the meter. Notice how Keats slows down the rhythm by loading some of his lines with emphasized syllables, often by using compounds with two such syllables in succession: "soft-dying," "full-grown," "Hedge-crickets," "red-breast." In the first example, "soft" is the final part of a **B ô B -o-** rhythmic figure which puts additional emphasis on "clouds bloom" and makes the lovely word "soft" a focus of attention, coming as it does where we expect an unemphasized syllable (so that the scansion of **"clouds bloom** the **soft"** is actually **B ô B -o=**).

The rhymes are a variation on the sonnet: a Shakespearean style quatrain is followed by a Petrarchan style sestet into which an unexpected third "-oft" rhyme has been introduced (with "croft") – further enhancing a sense of fullness, even as Keats describes the hints of winter to come.

7. The first of the four sections of Matthew Arnold's "Dover Beach."

Iambic lines of varied lengths, with rhyme (all perfect, or full, rhymes – like "night–light" – except for the "fair–air–roar" grouping, with "roar" being an imperfect, or half, rhyme).

The first three sentences, in which the speaker surveys the spectacle of the English Channel at night and invites his companion to join him, consist of a three-beat line followed by a four-beat line and then four five-beat lines. They are all iambic, and (after the very simple first line) use many of the usual rhythmic figures: **B O B** ("moon lies fair"), **-o- B ô B** ("on the French coast"; "is the night-air"), **B -o- B**, both initial ("Gleams and is gone"; "Glimmering and vast"; "Come to the window") and medial ("out in the tran-"). The way the lines gradually increase in length, and then settle down into iambic pentameter verse, imply a certain stability of mood, although the use of rhythmic figures contributes to the intensity of the feelings conveyed. But the following line, in which "Only" signifies a shift in the speaker's mood, introduces an uncertainty into the meter: does it have four or five beats? Either way, it cannot be performed as a line of regular meter; we have to mold the words to suit our choice. The subsequent lines are quite clearly iambic, but the shifting between four and five beats and the continuing use of rhythmic figures contribute a sense of unease as "the eternal note of sadness" is brought in.

8. Gerard Manley Hopkins's "Spring and Fall: to a young child."

Four-beat lines, predominantly trochaic – though considering the presence of iambic lines, and the unusual markings Hopkins uses to control the reader's performance, we'd call this stress verse. (One sure sign of stress verse is the frequent use of virtual and implied offbeats *without* accompanying double offbeats.) The poet himself called it by a name he invented: "sprung rhythm."

With attention to Hopkins's accentings, here is our scansion of this memorable poem. Note, by the way, that Hopkins insists that "is" in the next-to-last line – "It ís the blíght" – must be emphasized, as the most direct hint that "the name" of "the blight" is something like "mortality," "the passage of time," "death," or the Fall of humankind into sin. Note then how in the last line the more expected emphasis on "It" allows the poem to conclude with a calm, if melancholy, regularity.

```
Márgarét, áre you gríeving
 B  o B[o]B    o   B o

Over Goldengrove unleaving?
B o   B o   B  o B o

Leáves, líke the thíngs of mán, you
  B  [o]  B    o   B    o   B    o

With your fresh thoughts care for, can you?
  b    o     B      O        B   o   B  o

Áh! ás the héart grows ólder                    5
B[o]B   o  B       O   B o

It will come to such sights colder
b   o    B    o B    O       B o

By and by, nor spare a sigh
 B o    B   o    B   o B

Though worlds of wanwood leafmeal lie;
   o     B      o  B   o    B   o    B

And yet you *will* weep and know why.
o   B   o   B   ô B    -o=       B

Now no matter, child, the name:                10
 B  o  B o     B    o B

Sórrow's spríngs áre the sáme.
 B   o       B   ôB    o  B
```

```
Nor mouth had, no nor mind, expressed
 o  B    O   B  o  B   o  B
What héart héard of, ghóst guéssed:
 o  B   ôB    o    Bô B
It ís the blíght mán was bórn for,
o B   o  B    ôB  o   B   o
It is Margaret you mourn for.                    15
b o  B  oB   o   B    o
```

Hopkins's invented words are usually defined this way: "Goldengrove" suggests a grove of trees whose yellow autumn leaves are falling (un-leaf-ing); "wanwood" combines the word "wan," meaning tired or pale, with "wood"; and "leafmeal" suggests leaves being scattered gradually, one after another – that is, "piecemeal" – as well as the mealy substance they turn into.

We've mentioned that Hopkins felt it necessary to add emphasis marks (many or most of which, incidentally, are usually omitted when the poem is reprinted). But just why did he feel the poem required them? The answer may lie in the fact that if the marks are *not* there, the reader-performer may very well proceed for at least seven lines in a *three-beat* poem. To hear this alternative performance, remember that "Margaret" has two pronunciations: "Mar-ga-ret" and "Mar-grit." A performance that begins with the two-syllable version of the child's name speeds the poem up in a way that diminishes the power of what is being said, even to the point where those unusual rhymes "man, you/can you?" – passionate in the emphatic four-beat perfor-mance – become almost comic:

```
Margaret, are you grieving
 B   o   b   o   B  o
Over Goldengrove unleaving?
-o-  B  o   B  o B  o
Leaves, like the things of man, you
 B        -o-   B   o  B    o
With your fresh thoughts care for, can you?
  -o-     B    O      B   o   B   o
```

```
Ah! as the heart grows older                                    5
B   -o-    B      o   B  o

It will come to such sights colder . . .
  -o-     B    o B    O     B  o
```

And the italicized "*will*" serves to prevent line 9 from inviting this inappropriately quick three-beat performance:

```
And yet you will weep and know why.
 o   B   -o-   B     -o=     B
```

Another answer is that although many of the lines contain the eight syllables found in strict tetrameter poems, and many have seven syllables (common enough in four-beat poems), two of the lines, "Sorrow's springs are the same" and "What heart heard of, ghost guessed," have only *six* syllables. Without guidance (at least with the opening lines, to establish the four-beat norm), few readers could dependably, on their own, achieve the performance Hopkins intended.

9. The first stanza of Thomas Hardy's "Thoughts of Phena."

Anapestic trimeter, dimeter, and pentameter lines rhyming **ababcdcd**.

Thomas Hardy wrote poems in a great variety of metrical forms, but it's somewhat surprising to find a poem which grieves for a woman he loved written in a meter which continually calls attention to its thumping beat. Moreover, in this first stanza and later stanzas as well, there is a forced quality to some of the rhymes (like "light" and "unsight") and some of the word orderings. (It takes a moment to realize that in the last line the poet is saying "her eyes were upbrimming with laughter.") And the sequence of rhythmical lines – three-beat, two-beat, and strangely long five-beat – is disconcerting. We have asked ourselves, and you might ask yourself, what is the effect of the poet's using this prominent meter in unexpected and even wrenching patterns? Is perhaps the depth of his grief being expressed by the evident struggle to put these anguishing memories and regrets into an insistent meter – a meter whose obviousness and regularity provide some solace for feelings otherwise beyond control?

Here is a likely performance:

```
    Not a line of her writing have I,
     -o-  B    -o-     B  -o-    B
      Not a thread of her hair,
       -o-   B   -o-   B
  No mark of her late time as dame in her dwelling, whereby
   o B   -o-   B    =o-  B   -o-    B   -o-     B
      I may picture her there;
       -o-  B   -o-    B
    And in vain do I urge my unsight              5
     -o-  B   -o- B    -o=  B
      To conceive my lost prize
       -o-   B    -o=    B
  At her close whom I knew when her dreams were
   -o-   B     -o-   B   -o-    B     -o-
                        upbrimming with light,
                         B    -o-   B
  And with laughter her eyes.
   -o-    B    -o-   B
```

10. Section four of T. S. Eliot's "Burnt Norton."

Initially, stress verse with rhyme; then, free verse.

One interesting feature of Eliot's rhythms is the way that identifiable metrical patterns frequently underlie lines that could be taken for free verse. Lines 1, 2, and 4 have four beats ("cloud" being an emphasized offbeat) and share the rhyme; in the four-beat context, line 3 may be sensed as four beats, too. But a five-beat performance of that line is certainly a possibility; and since the strong metricality disappears as the stanza concludes, either possibility is about as good as the other – if indeed line 3 is felt to *have* a meter. After the breakdown of the meter in lines 5 and 6, a fairly regular duple rhythm is established, though there is no consistency in line-length. The rhymes keep coming, however.

By drawing on, but not wholly accepting, traditional meters, Eliot is able to convey the connections between his poetry and that of the extensive tradition of poetry in English, whether the almost nursery-rhyme-like quality of the opening couplet that makes the imagery all the more macabre, or the shadow of the iambic pentameter that haunts the last three lines to imbue their philosophical speculation with added gravity. It's easy to turn the last two lines into fairly regular pentameters by moving the two words "is still":

```
Has answered light to light, and is silent, the light
 o  B   o    B    o B     -o-  B   -o-   B

Is still at the still point of the turning world.
o   B   -o-   B ô B    -o-   B  o   B
```

11. The first two stanzas and the last stanza of Elizabeth Bishop's "One Art."

Iambic pentameter with rhyme.

The form Bishop uses is a very old French one, the villanelle. "One Art" has the villanelle's five traditional three-line stanzas followed by a concluding four-line one, with repetitions (somewhat varied) of lines one and three from the first stanza.

The requirements of the villanelle's form – including, in the English version, strict iambic pentameter – seem almost a help to the poet who is trying to come to terms with chaotic emotions caused by the loss of another's love. After several stanzas where places, names, her mother's watch, and "some realms I owned" are lost sadly but not terribly, the final stanza speaks intimately to "you," to the loved one. And in the final line – with parentheses, italics, and an exclamation point (*Write* it!) – the poet seems at last to find the strength to say, powerfully, that the loss of this person's love is indeed an *almost*-unspeakable disaster.

12. John Agard's "Is More Than a Snapshot Mirror."

Iambic trimeter (though with several lines most likely performed by a reader as tetrameters), with irregular half and full rhymes.

The poem encapsulates the cultural and historical importance of steel band music to those who perform it and love it. There is no mistaking its metricality, and its rhythms suggest a truth about it: it moves with the feeling of the steel drum music which is its subject. Even the slashes, which suggest pauses that give extra emphasis to the words separated by them, like "straw," "hat," and "native" in line five, contribute a feeling of metricality to a spoken or sung performance (though like punctuation generally, slashes do not of themselves indicate virtual offbeats, even though certain ones coincide with such offbeats).

We have been lucky enough to hear a recorded reading of the poem by John Agard himself, and can report that the poet uses a three-beat line with very clear emphases, though the regularity is interestingly varied with pauses and changing tempos; there's also an approach to a tune at times. Even the last two lines become three-beat in Agard's performance.

However, in our first readings of the poem, we sensed some rhythms differently from Agard, and our own performances differed. Tom clearly felt four beats in line 9 (Is **more** than **knock**ing **out** a **tune**), while Derek felt three (Is **more** than **knock**ing out a **tune**); and both of us experienced four beats in the last line (is a **heap** of **his**tory **in** you **hand** – with more than minimal emphasis on "in"). But we weren't disturbed that our two performances were not identical and, in fact, were different from the author's three-beat norm. Hearing the final line, for example, as either four or three beats still resulted in strongly felt lines which energetically conveyed a conviction that the pan is not simply a polished, mirror-like drum which Caribbean musicians play to entertain tourists: it is an emblem of a culture. One can experience this sense of conviction in the three strong emphases on "heap," on "history," and on the "hand" of those who play pans – the emphases heightened by the alliteration of the "h" sound. The alternative performance is equally strong though somewhat different in meaning: when four beats include emphasis on "in," the line becomes a demonstration of the possessive feeling for this musical art which lives in its players' hands.

Here, though, is the poet's own performance, as we have heard it:

```
Is more than a snapshot mirror
o  B      -o-  B  o  B o [B]

reflecting panman face
 o B o   B o   B  [B]

in a mood of concentration
 -o-  B  o   b  o  B o [B]

complete with perspiration
 o  B   o   b  oB o [B]
```

```
Is more than a straw / hat / native                          5
o  B        -o-    B    O    B o  [B]

making a merry steel show
 B  -o-  B  -o=       B  [B]

whilst he catching ass to live
    -o-    B   o  B   o  B   [B]

in some bad / john / ghetto
-o-     B [o] B  [o]  B  o [B]


Is more than knocking out a tune
o  B   o   B      ~o~     B  [B]

on a sunbeach / package / tour                               10
 -o- B  o       B  o     B  [B]

with rum flowing like blood
o   B ô B  -o-      B  [B]

and the body calling for more
 -o-     B o B   -o-    B   [B]


No/
 B  [B]

pan deeper than that man
 B ô B      ~o~      B  [B]

            is a heap of history in you hand     15
            -o-  B  o  B     ~o~     B   [B]
```

Our scansion here is doing something a little different from what it does in earlier examples: it serves to record a particular performance emerging partly from the rhythms of speech (as in all the poems we have discussed) and partly from a musical rhythm to which the words are molded. Imagine the drums accompanying the poem: they would bring out the musical rhythm which the words sometimes duplicate, sometimes pull against, just as the accompaniment in rap music plays a complicated duet with the rhythmic speech of its performer. Once the poem originally composed for spoken or musical presentation is circulated in written form, the reader is of course free to discover the rhythms of its language. Agard's last stanza can then be sensed as something different from the one the poet recorded. The steel drum dates back to the 1940s, and when its history is referred to in a concluding line of four beats – the simplest of English meters – the pan and all it stands for indeed become deeper than any single person. The metrical line itself can be taken to represent the connection between a people's need for expression and those deeply felt rhythms which have traditionally served to embody it.

13. Paul Muldoon's "The Train."
A poem clearly modeled on the form of sonnets encountered earlier, with fourteen lines and with rhymes (mostly imperfect) occurring in couplet pairs.

In our performances of "The Train" we've felt waverings between four-beat lines with many double and triple offbeats (a casual reading), and five-beat lines with many implied and virtual offbeats (an emphatic reading).

To come to terms with the poet's emphases and meanings, we tried out two scansions based on the two possibilities which had suggested themselves: a tetrameter norm and a pentameter norm. Both seem somewhat forced and unsatisfactory in certain respects, but having completed the exercise, we feel we can make a statement about what is going on rhythmically which we could not make without having gone through the process. Here are the two scansions, which you can perform for yourself, feeling the differences.

The four-beat-norm version (which we'll call the conversational sonnet):

```
I've been trying, my darling, to explain
  -o-      B   -o-   B   o     b o   B
to myself how it is that some freight train
-o- B    -o-  B    o   B     O       B
loaded with ballast so a track may rest
B    -o-     B     ~o~    B    o   B
easier in its bed should be what's roused
B    ~o~     B    o     B   o    B
us both from ours, tonight as every night,        5
o   B    o  B     o B      ~o~     B
despite its being miles off and despite
  o  B   o    B  -o=    B    -o-   B
```

```
our custom of putting to the very
o    B   -o-   B  o    b   o  B o

back of the mind all that's customary
 B     -o-    B    -o-    B  o b o

and then, since it takes forever to pass
o     B       -o-   B    o B -o-   B

with its car after car of coal and gas        10
  -o-    B  -o-   B  o  B   o    B

and salt and wheat and rails and railway ties,
o   B   o    B   o    B       ~o~      B

how it seems determined to give the lie
 -o-   B    o B     -o-   B    o  B

to the notion, my darling,
-o-    B   -o-    B  o

that we, not it, might be the constant thing.
 o  B   o  B        ~o~      B   o    B
```

Now the five-beat-norm version (which we'll call the anguished
sonnet):

```
I've been trying, my darling, to explain
B    o    B   -o-   B  o    b o   B

to myself how it is that some freight train
-o-  B  ô B  o  B   o    B    O      B

loaded with ballast so a track may rest
 B   -o-    B   o   b o  B   o    B

easier in its bed should be what's roused
B   o  b o   B    o    B   o    B

us both from ours, tonight as every night,        5
O   B    o   B      o B   o  B   o  B

despite its being miles off and despite
 o  B   o   bo   B   ôB    -o-    B

our custom of putting to the very
B  ô B   -o-   B  o    b  o  B o
```

```
back of the mind all that's customary
B   -o-   B  ôB    o     B  o b o

and then, since it takes forever to pass
o    B [o]B   o  B    o B -o-   B

with its car after car of coal and gas          10
B   o    B   -o-   B  o   B  o   B

and salt and wheat and rails and railway ties,
o   B  o    B    o   B   o   B   o   B

how it seems determined to give the lie
B  o   B    o B    -o-    B   o  B

to the notion, my darling,
b   o  B   -o-    B  o

that we, not it, might be the constant thing.
o    B   o  B [o]B    -o-     B  o     B
```

Naturally, for this exercise, we tried to hear and scan the lines consistently, as being four or five beats. We doubt, though, that the author intended either as the poem's norm – a more casual mix seems likely. Nevertheless, in whatever manner the lines are felt, the mixture itself contributes to the poem's metrical representation of feeling. So here's the conclusion we came to: the poem's wavering between two ways of feeling the meter reflects anxiety, as the speaker questions whether human love can indeed be – as it sometimes seems to be – unwavering, or whether only the unsettling invasion of their bedroom by a train's noise is "the constant thing." Muldoon exploits the freedom to settle into a firmly regular rhythm to give point to certain lines, notably when the rhythm of the verse evokes the apparently endless rhythmic sounds of the distant passing train in the tenth and eleventh lines, most easily heard as a four-beat line followed by a five-beat line. The final line, too, has more rhythmic stability than most – it's an entirely regular iambic pentameter – and helps to give the sonnet (and its single long sentence) a firm sense of closure as well as hinting at the constancy which has been mysteriously transferred to the noise of the train.

What are your feelings about the poem's statements, taking into account not only what is said, but the possible rhythms in which the statements are made? If you were to write out a single scansion of your own performance of "The Train," would it more closely approach a four- or five-beat norm? Even taking into account the surprisingly short penultimate line (what is its effect?), it seems clear that this contemporary poet is exploiting a range of metrical effects to enlarge the meanings of his poem.

WHERE TO GO FROM HERE

When you have worked your way through this book, reading all the examples aloud and trying out all the exercises, you will have a good grasp of the way English meter works. The next step is to use this ability to increase your enjoyment of the poems you encounter from now on. You don't have to scan every poem in regular meter that you read; scanning is a useful activity to get fully involved with a poet's use of rhythm, but if you've understood what we have explained here – understood not just with the brain but with ears and body too – the payoff will come each time you read a poem (aloud, whenever possible). Without having to think consciously about it, your mind and muscles will register the patterns of beats and offbeats, you will recognize the familiar rhythmic figures, your voice will make the slight adjustments needed to bring out the meter without imposing it on the words. And all these activities will feed into your sense of what the poem is doing: the meanings it's exploring, the emotions it's conveying, the way it unfolds as an event of language – a meditation, an appeal, a memory, an argument, a story, a drama.

If, however, you want to find out more about the ways poets have used, and continue to use, rhythm, you could investigate two books by one of this book's authors, Derek Attridge: *Poetic Rhythm: An Introduction* (Cambridge University Press, 1995) and *The Rhythms of English Poetry* (Longman, 1982). The first of these examines matters beyond those discussed in this book and provides many more exercises to work through. It analyzes the elements out of which English verse is made – syllables and their accents – and explains more fully how the patterns in English poetry arise out of a combination of two things: the way the language is spoken and the way the mind and body respond to simple rhythms. In addition to examining the sorts of metrical verse we've focused on, *Poetic Rhythm* explores stress verse and strong-stress verse (such as Anglo-Saxon verse and rap), and different types of free verse. One chapter suggests a way of scanning the movements of syntax in a poem – the rhythms produced by phrases and sentences. The second book, *The Rhythms of English Poetry*, is longer and more scholarly. As well as elaborating beat prosody in detail, it surveys a wide range of approaches to the question of meter, assessing the merits and limitations of traditional foot-scansion and certain contemporary generative approaches to English meter. (These two books use somewhat different symbols for scansion, but having learned those of *Meter and Meaning*, you'll have no trouble using them. See "Scansion Symbols" below for a comparative table.)

Though there are numerous other introductions, manuals, and reference works that deal with English meter, nearly all of them see as their task the exposition and justification of the terms used in foot-prosody – terms invented for Ancient Greek verse and adapted by the Romans for the scansion of Latin verse, and later taken over to describe the meters of English poetry. It is, however, advantageous to know the most common of these terms, since they are used in many works of criticism. If you want to go beyond the brief introduction to the terms we have given in our "Names and Labels" chapter, the handiest and most readable account is provided by John Hollander (himself a fine poet) in *Rhyme's Reason: A Guide to English Verse* (Yale University Press, 1981; later revised editions). John Hollander is also the author of *Vision and Resonance: Two Senses of Poetic Form* (Yale University Press, 1975, 1985), a book of criticism that shows how much insight into poetry can be obtained by a sensitive examination of details of rhythm and meter.

SCANSION SYMBOLS

RULE

Meter in English poetry is realized by the alternation of beats and offbeats.

RHYTHM MARKERS

(*below* the line of verse)

B   beat [emphasized syllable]
b   beat [unemphasized syllable]
[B] virtual beat [no syllable]
         (perceived at the ends of trimeter lines, as in ballad stanzas)
o   offbeat [unemphasized syllable]
O   offbeat [emphasized syllable]
-o- double offbeat [two unemphasized syllables]
         (one – very rarely, both – of the two syllables that comprise an offbeat may be emphasized (=): =o-, -o=, =o=)
[o] virtual offbeat [no syllable, perceived offbeat]
ô   implied offbeat [no syllable, necessary rhythmical pause][1]
~o~ triple offbeat [three unemphasized syllables]
         (exceedingly rare in stricter metrical styles)

RHYTHMIC FIGURES

(**#** = beginning or end of line; **//** = significant break in the line)

1. **o b o**
   o b #
   # b o
   Unemphasized syllable functioning as beat (often called "promotion")

2. **B O B**
   # O B
   Emphasized syllable functioning as offbeat (often called "demotion")

3. **# B -o- B**
   // B -o- B
   Double offbeat between beats at the beginning of a line ("initial inversion") or after a significant break ("medial inversion")

4. **-o- B ô B**
   Double offbeat followed by beat, implied offbeat, beat ("offbeat-initial pairing")

5. **B ô B -o-**
   Beat, implied offbeat, beat followed by double offbeat ("beat-initial pairing")

EQUIVALENT SYMBOLS

Symbol systems for beat-offbeat scansion have evolved to meet differing needs, though all are currently in use. The symbols used in *Meter and Meaning* are easy to type or write variants of the **B**'s and **o**'s in Derek Attridge's *The Rhythms of English Poetry* (Longman, 1982). For those wishing to explore *The Rhythms of English Poetry* or the same author's *Poetic Rhythm: An Introduction* (Cambridge, 1995), the following conversion chart may be useful.

	M&M	REP	PR
emphasized beat	B	B	$\underline{/}$
unemphasized beat	b	B̄	$\underline{x}$
virtual beat	[B]	[B]	[$\underline{/}$]
unemphasized offbeat	o	o	x
emphasized offbeat	O	ò	/
double offbeat[2]	-o-	ŏ	x x
virtual offbeat[3]	[o]	ô	[x]
implied offbeat[3]	ô	ô	
triple offbeat	~o~	ŏ	x x x

NOTES

1 You may find it useful to know that the ô symbol can be found in the set of symbols available in many word-processing programs, or you can insert it by holding down the ALT key and entering the number 147 on the numeric keypad. In some programs (such as Word) you can achieve the same result by holding down the Ctrl and Shift keys and typing ^, then releasing those keys and typing o. Alternatively, you may wish to use the somewhat less elegant symbol o^.

2 Here are the symbols used in the three books for variants of the double offbeat, indicating a double offbeat with the first part emphasized, the second part, and both parts:

M&M   =o-   -o=   =o=
REP   ŏ   ŏ   ö
PR   /x   x/   //

3 *The Rhythms of English Poetry* does not distinguish between virtual and implied offbeats; both kinds are called "implied." (The only exceptions are virtual offbeats which occur with virtual beats – called "unrealized" beats in *REP* – and are shown with them: [oB].) *Poetic Rhythm* does distinguish between virtual and implied offbeats, and shows implied offbeats by means of two successive emphasized beats ($\underline{//}$), where an implied offbeat is always assumed to occur between the beats.

AFTERWORD

Meters: Watching the Snow Geese from the Banks of the St. Lawrence at Montmagny, Québec

I

Their powerful wings
Have beat through the night;
The migration brings
These thousands in flight

Where atmosphere sings
As down from that height
The snow geese, in rings,
Descend and alight.

II

Low over marshy waters fly
The geese, while here I stand
Watching their shadows magnify
Moments before they land.

Then every foraging family
Voices ancestral sound,
Perpetuating harmony
Heard all the world around.

III

The patterns of their flight – the orderings
Of arrows in the sky – are not by chance;
An annual cycle of existence brings
Its form to every day's experience
Until, with custom structuring their lives,
The habits grow by which the flock survives.

And we, who occupy this time and space
With these magnificent masters of the air,
May find in cadenced language our own place
Where subtly measured meanings let us share
Those rhythms which, embedded at our birth,
Are sensed as steady heartbeats of the earth.

Thomas Carper

INDEX OF POETS AND POEMS